YOU AND THE MUSIC BUSINESS

EMPOWERING INDEPENDENT ARTISTS
A Self-Care Guide to Finding Balance
and Joy in Today's Music Industry

LIFE COACHING FOR MUSIC MAKERS

TARA SHANNON

YOU AND THE MUSIC BUSINESS

EMPOWERING INDEPENDENT ARTISTS: A SELF-CARE GUIDE TO FINDING BALANCE AND JOY IN TODAY'S MUSIC INDUSTRY

TARA SHANNON

Lucky Book Publishing

Copyright © 2023 Tara Shannon Renaud

Published by Lucky Book Publishing: www.luckybookpublishing.com

All rights reserved. No part of this book may be reproduced or used in any manner without the prior written permission of the copyright owner, except for the use of brief quotations in a book review.

The author does not dispense medical advice or prescribe the use of any technique as a form of treatment for physical, emotional or medical problems without the advice of a physician, either directly or indirectly. The intent of the author is only to offer information of a general true nature to help you in your quest for emotional, physical and spiritual well-being. In the event you use any of the information in this book for yourself, the author and the publisher assume no responsibility for your actions.

To request permissions, contact the publisher at hello@luckybookpublishing.com.

Paperback ISBN: 978-1-7388227-3-7
Hardcover ISBN: 978-1-7388227-4-4
E-book ISBN: 978-1-7388227-5-1

1st edition, July 2023.

PRAISE FOR YOU AND THE MUSIC BUSINESS

"This is an essential interactive guide for all musicians who have ever forgotten why they got into music, experienced imposter syndrome, or felt like the industry wants something different than who they are.... so pretty much every musician."

- BYRON PASCOE, ENTERTAINMENT LAWYER & PARTNER, EDWARDS CREATIVE LAW

"This book is the perfect blend of nurturing guidance and hard truths. It will help you make an optimistic plan while also avoiding the pitfalls and setbacks that can slow down so many artists."

- STEVE FOLEY, PRODUCER/ENGINEER, KELLYLEE EVANS, THE COOPER BROTHERS, 6 TIME JUNO WINNER KEITH GLASS

"This book is a game-changer in music literature. It revolutionizes how we navigate the industry as music creators, combining self-care strategies and a deep understanding of ourselves with a business mindset. Everyone should read this book!"

- MELANIE BRULÉE, EXECUTIVE DIRECTOR OTTAWA MUSIC INDUSTRY COALITION

"Read YOU and the Music Business. It's a positive jolt of finding your inner self. This will help you find your place in today's music business. Inspiring!"

- DALE PETERS, PRESIDENT, DALE SPEAKING

'This book is the next best thing to sitting down with an artist to have a conversation about the music industry. Even better, while focused on the business of music, the gems Tara offers will resonate with independent artists in other fields. Bottom line, if you're an indie artist looking for a mentor, Tara's book is a must read."

- ALASTAIR LUFT, AUTHOR/SPEAKER, 2019 PENCRAFT AWARDS FINALIST, 20 YEAR VETERAN CANADIAN ARMED FORCES

"Tara's book about 'YOU and the Music Business" is replete with pertinent strategies for personal, self-understanding and the fundamentals necessary for a successful career experience in the music creation business. What Tara outlines throughout the book is made even more credible to the reader by the fact that she has lived each belief and strategy both in music and business. She is joyfully describing her authentic, artistic journey from student to mentor to the benefit of countless artists."

— **ALAN & GEORGIA MORISSETTE,** *INTEGRITY TALENT DIRECTION*

"Tara Shannon turns the self-help, music industry business guide onto its head. She urges music creators to look within, rather than outside, to identify and deconstruct their dreams and career goals. She helps quell the external noise and focuses on the true art of creating music and then provides no-nonsense advice on how to make a living from one's art. Because she writes the way she speaks, with authenticity, this book reads like an intimate coaching session. It's sure to become a trusted source and reference for art and music creators everywhere. Just as she is in person, she is very generous in sharing her insights, knowledge and decades of learned experience. Everyone needs a Tara Shannon in their lives. If you don't have one, you'll want to keep this guide in your back pocket."

- **ANNE-MARIE BRUGGER,** *CHUO RADIO BROADCASTER, ARTS REPORTER & EMERGING ARTIST ADVOCATE FOR OVER 20 YEARS*

"This is a book for all artists. It's a backstage pass to the wild world of music and how to navigate the business as an independent artist. It's like having a wiser, funnier bandmate to guide you through the chaos. The book is a lot like a backstage therapy session, complete with tales and juicy tidbits on surviving the madness."

- **LOGAN MILLER,** *FOUNDER AND MARKETING DIRECTOR FRONT PORCH MUSIC + MARKETING*

"This book is a big, warm, encouraging hug from your music industry fairy Godmother. It is beautifully written and reads as a firm yet gentle conversation with a trusted mentor. While shining a light on the realities of the industry, it reignites the fire within reminding you that your art and craft matter; you matter. This book serves as a handy and helpful tool to not only musical artists but any professional in any artistic field; validating your feelings while empowering you to take ownership of your business and encouraging you to look inward, reevaluate your perspective, and give yourself permission to fall in love with this dream all over again."

- SAM STONE, *SONGWRITER, INDEPENDENT ARTIST*

"Tara's book is a lean, yet sweeping crash course on the music business and how to be as you pass through it. Artists need books like this one as it strikes the nuanced balance of being clear-eyed and sober with compassion and encouragement."

- PATRICK ERMLICH, *GRAMOPHONE MEDIA / COMPASS METHOD CONSULTING*

"It's very difficult for me to write a review for this book. Not because I don't have the words, but because I have TOO many! Not only is this book a must have for artists, no matter what stage you're at in your career, it helps you gain a deeper understanding and connection to who you are. A real, raw and never before written perspective on the music business, creativity, and your inner self. Do yourself a favour, read this book, and let your true artist shine."

- JESSICA PEARSON AND THE EAST WIND, *SONGWRITER, INDEPENDENT ARTIST*

"Tara's words are the key to unlocking both power and peace inside yourself as an artist. The reality of business swirls together with inspiration, curiosity and the connection to your inner self. As a songwriter, artist and music creator this book is the deep breath of truth you've been looking for."

- MIKAYLA MENZIES, *SONGWRITER, INDEPENDENT ARTIST*

"Your vision will become clear only when you can look into your own heart. Who looks outside, dreams; who looks inside, awakes."

~ CARL JUNG

ACKNOWLEDGMENTS

I dedicate this book to every creator out there who is bravely charting their own dance with music.

To my beautiful amazing children, you are an ongoing inspiration and a reminder for me to be the best version of myself that I can be. I love you all.

To Sam, Jessica & Mikayla, it's an honor and a privilege to work with you every day. You make me better. And I am so grateful.

To Byron, I'm not sure I would have ever finished this book without the loving nudges from you along the way. Thank you.

To my friends and family, you have supported me and loved me through all the crazy. I've been able to step into the fullness of who I am because of it. I am so lucky to be so loved.

To my music industry community, I was a little late to the party after raising so many kids, but when the time came and I could dedicate myself to my career as a professional in music, you welcomed me in and offered a seat at the table. I will forever be grateful for the mentoring and kindness I have been given and continue to receive.

To my publishing team, Samantha & Simar, how amazing is the universe? A chance encounter at a charity event led to an incredible experience with you learning about this world of book publishing. You are exactly the team my heart asked for. You have guided me and inspired me to believe that I am indeed an author. What a privilege it is to be in such company. A million thank yous.

You have all helped me realize this vision and I am so, so grateful.

~ Tara xo

Get your free accompanying YOU and the Music Business Journal to download at www.gro-ve.com/journal

CONTENTS

Preface		xix
Introduction		xxiii
1.	Indie. Redefined	1
2.	The Creative Cycle	13
3.	The Core Principles Of Business	33
4.	Business is about People	45
5.	Money, Money, Money	61
6.	Look For The Helpers	73
7.	Caught In A Trap	91
8.	Purpose In All Things	103
9.	The Experience Of You	115
	Conclusion	133
	Author's Note	137
	Meet Tara Shannon	139
	Emotional Check In	141
	Mood Index	145
	Recommended Reading	147
	Thank You	149

PREFACE

Dear Music Creator,

The idea for this book has been bouncing around in my head for a while now. After thousands of hours coaching clients, I noticed a common pattern among us music creators. There is this tug of war inside each of us. I could see that we are all wrestling with the same demons: self-doubt, imposter syndrome, frustration, disillusionment, really high highs and really low lows. A common feeling of confusion in a world where being a music creator comes with so many mixed signals. Where reaching "success" as a music creator seems so elusive and reserved for the chosen.

I started to understand that we all feel this pull inside ourselves to create, but our minds wrestle with the conditioning of our culture...it's not a "real" job...you need a plan B...it's really hard to "make it"...you need to grow up now...on and on it goes...all of it pushing and pulling against the internal compulsion to create. Something so visceral, so real and sometimes all-consuming. We often find ourselves in a conflicted and vulnerable state, becoming easily influenced by what others think of us.

While also being influenced by the big music money machine. Conditioned to believe that true "success" only looks like stadium touring and hit songs on the radio. We find ourselves chasing dangling carrots: go here, do that, be this and then you'll be chosen. The voices in our head growing louder, creating so much noise that it becomes difficult to hear our own inner voice. In our own search to feel validated, we become vulnerable and develop a bad case of "if-i-tis."

What if I get discovered! I could be a star! What if that record exec hears my songs! What if so and so cuts my song! What if this is my one and only opportunity to make it! If only the right person hears my music, if only one of my songs got on the radio or got a million streams...everything will fall into place! I will finally make it. I will have arrived. Then I'll be a "real" artist.

I started to wonder why we all seemed to have this same tape playing over and over in our minds....where did these beliefs come from? Who is holding that dangling carrot stick watching us all dance to the illusion? When did we become so willing to give our power away, letting someone or something else determine when we and what we create are worthy?

And I noticed that when we are exhausted by the dance and make the eventual choice to leave music aside and get a "real" job, it never leaves us anyway. If she is a part of you, Music is always in us and around us. She is ever-present in our longing, our daydreams, our desires. It's both a blessing and a curse, and inevitably, she pulls us back to her. Because music is just part of our DNA...it's woven into the fabric of who we are and there is no escape. We cannot run from ourselves.

And so then the question becomes, how do we, inside ourselves, validate the pursuit of it? How do we justify the creation of music in our lives as a credible part of us? How do we move forward in knowing that what we create matters?

Whether we sing the only song we've ever written to our mom in the kitchen or release a single that gets millions of streams, it all matters.

The power is in the knowing that seeking validation outside ourselves will never truly fulfill us. Turning inward for that sense of well-being is the power...because validation is in the creating itself. You are a creator! You are a conduit for the life force that flows through us all - for life itself. A channel for Source Energy and music is its language.

You matter.

What you create matters.

Simply because you are breathing.

Now, how to bring your music to the marketplace and make enough money to eat and pay your rent is part of the conversation in this book, but it is secondary. When you shift your focus from the external need for validation to the internal need for joy and purpose, you are truly free. Because how you feel when you create is all that really matters. The voices in your head that say you and your music are only worthy when someone listens, someone buys or someone "signs," can be silenced. Because we can choose. The endless pursuit of validation from outside yourself or the inner journey to a greater knowing <u>of</u> yourself.

This book is a method. A way of being while you navigate your life as a music creator. It's meant to be a guide back out of that rabbit hole when you feel yourself tumbling down. It's not a music business book per se, although business is really just about people, and the more you understand people, the better you are at business. And the only way to understand people is to understand yourself. And more specifically, understanding yourself as a music creator. So it is, in some ways, a music business book. But hopefully, more.

It is a path to YOU. Wonderful, amazing, powerful YOU.

So create my dear friends! Create. Unapologetically and with total abandon.

Let everything inside of you spill out into this big, beautiful world....that we may all get to know big and beautiful YOU.

~ Tara Shannon xo

INTRODUCTION

There are many wonderful music business books out there in the world. Many really good ones. The content is mostly focused on the current information about how the business works, the changes and trends, the dos and don'ts. And I love those books. I just love the music business - all the good and the bad - because it brings together my two favorite subjects: music and business. But mostly because both music and business are about the same thing - people. And I love people.

I feel the most joy in my life when I am being of service to people. When I am helping others. Writing another music industry book may have been helpful, but there are many very qualified people who have already done it and done it well. What I felt might be even more helpful is a guide that helps you to understand yourself as a person. Understanding yourself as a music creator IN today's music industry so that you can find your own version of success on this journey with music in your life. Because it's not an easy journey. It's not easy living with the gift of music inside of you with no clear path on how to use that gift to make a living.

I wanted to create something that might help you find a sense of peace when you might need it. Help encourage you when you feel down. And celebrate with you when something goes right! This book will give you some insights on how the business works, yes, but from the perspective of who YOU are and how to define your personal relationship with music. Because loving music is both a blessing and a curse. It can be all-consuming. Blissful. And torturous. When music is a part of who you are, you need a place to express it. And in a culture where we are sold the dream of being a star as the only definition of success, we are often left confused and disoriented when becoming said star is not happening or might not even be an option.

Music is a hobby for most - an expensive one at that. It's a challenging thing to have something woven into the DNA of who we are in a culture that defines success through income. When the music we make does not make money, we can be left feeling like a failure.

I wanted to share the lessons I've learned along the way that helped me redefine my own version of success. My own ways of feeling validated and purposeful as a music creator apart from any income my music may or may not bring in. Creating music is a way of life and if it lives within you, knowing how to balance your life around music is helpful. It was for me. I had to learn to realign my sense of self and my feeling of self worth and come to a deeper understanding of the purpose of music in my life. And it was a long road.

My Dance With Music

When I was seven years old, I started piano lessons, and Music asked me to dance. Strong and steady, she taught me the 12 steps, always helping me find the one - keeping time for me. I knew that Music and I would be lifelong partners...and we danced and danced until I was 18 - when I found out I was going to be a young mother. So I let go. I stopped dancing. I couldn't hear Music calling out the steps to me anymore, and I was lost in the silence.

But when my baby's newborn cries echoed, it was the sweetest sound, and the steady beat of his heart against mine stirred up rhythm. Melody soon followed. Then Suite no. 1 became the Seven Movement Symphony. Music and I danced and danced.

When Necessity tapped Music on the shoulder, asking to cut in...I obliged. So, Music left, and I tried falling into step under the demands of Necessity. But I was two left feet tripping over quarters and I could not find my groove. I was off balance and my head was spinning ...I could feel myself slipping so I let go. I let go so that I could steady my heart. And find my feet again. I needed my other partner back. I searched the room but couldn't hear her....I thought for sure Music had left. Then I looked up....and I felt her. Smiling... patiently waiting.

Is it my turn again? She sang.

Yes...it finally is.

Shall we?

MY STORY

I fell in love with music from the start. As a 7-year-old, I started taking piano lessons from a wonderful lady in our neighborhood, Madame Rita Massé. I still remember the smell of her house. And she was always dressed to the nines. She was French and loved to cook. There was always something in the oven or on the stove when I showed up for my lesson. She was very kind to me but very strict. I studied through the Royal Conservatory of Music, and I think she was nice to me because she thought I had talent. I could hear her with other students sometimes if I arrived early for my lesson, and she was not as nice. I remember her saying to my mother, who doesn't speak a word of French, that I was *douée*. My mother smiled and thanked her and then asked me in the car what she meant. She said, "I am gifted," which made my mom smile.

I loved to play, and so I actually practiced. And I loved music in all forms. I loved to sing in the church choir, and I eventually picked up the saxophone in high school and became solo chair in the jazz band. Luckily at my high school, it was very cool to be in the band. My teacher Mr. Pierre Vaillancourt had a lot of faith in me, and with his guidance, I ended up with early acceptance to an honors program in music at McGill University. Music was my everything. And I was going to build a career as a musician, work in music therapy or maybe become a music teacher.

When I was at McGill, I wrote my first song. My cousin was getting married, and I wanted to do something special for her. So I sat down and wrote my very first song. Side note - it's a super bad idea to present someone with an original song on such a special day; it could have gone horribly wrong, and I don't recommend it. But luckily, it wasn't terrible and she loved it, and it did make her feel special.

The moment when I shared something that I wrote with an audience, I was done for. I fell in love with music in a whole new way. I now had this incredible outlet to share my thoughts and feelings about life as I experienced it. A way to process hurt and wonder. In that moment, I knew that writing songs and singing for people was my purpose. So now I had to figure out what a life writing songs looked like. Back then, every piece of advice pointed to "you need a record deal" or "you need a publishing deal." I had no idea what that meant or how to get one, but it was my new focus.

I was also a young mother, and so balancing this new pursuit with the demands of motherhood in a new marriage was challenging. Especially because I understood nothing of what I was chasing. With a partner who was a realist and not a dreamer. But I was determined.

I kept writing and releasing music with the help of family, friends and the small community I lived in. I was building a small audience and performing when and where I could manage. A series of events led to me getting that elusive record deal offer with a small label out of Toronto. But in the discussions, it became clear what would be expected of me. And it became equally clear that I was unable to do any of it as a young mother of three boys. I didn't want to leave them to go on tour. I didn't want to be on the road constantly. I didn't want to be away from my family and friends.

Now this was back before the internet and social media, so there really was only one way to build your audience, and raising a young family as a new developing artist did not align well with the strategy. I knew in that moment that my first purpose was motherhood, and a recording career would have to take a back seat for a while. With a new understanding of what it actually meant to be a recording and touring artist, I focused more on just the songwriting, which I could more easily do from home while raising littles.

I always had a mind for business though, too.

From my earliest memories, I was always wired to see how I could make money. When I was around seven, we had this majestic chestnut tree in our front yard, and when the chestnuts fell in the fall, I remember thinking it was such waste. And so I made necklaces out of them. I would paint them and ask my dad to drill holes in them so I could thread colored yarn through them. And then I set out to sell them to the neighbors. A lemonade stand would have been so much easier. But I was wired to solve problems. The chestnuts were going to waste, and that was a problem to solve. And a potential opportunity.

When I was 16, my dad helped me buy a used car with my waitressing tips, and I started a little business called "Music Matters" in which my service was to come to your home to give music lessons. This home service was appealing because we lived in the country, and not every family could bring their kids into town for lessons. I saw a problem to solve and a need no one else was meeting *et voila*. I'm in business.

The problem I was trying to solve as a paused recording artist now turned songwriter was how to make money writing songs. I also realized that I liked finding ways to use music to raise awareness and build community. When I was approached by an organization to write a theme song and put together an album project to help them raise funds by selling the CDs, I discovered a way to marry all my skills. It was the perfect blend of my love for music, my love of business and my love for people. And so I focused on writing songs in partnership with organizations to help raise funds or awareness, as well as running my music school, which now had four teachers and over a hundred students.

Looking back now, I see the pattern so clearly. Music was going to be in my life one way or another. And for me, as long as it was making money, it was justifiable. Making music for myself as an artist was not justifiable because it cost money and didn't necessarily make money. It was deeply ingrained in me that, if something wasn't making money, it was a waste. And foolish.

Eventually, with the expansion of my family (I have five sons and two daughters), music had to be put aside entirely. The demands of raising a family of competitive hockey players took over, and my life became a blur of hockey rinks and growing a business in the transportation industry with their father.

No more music. The music creator in me laid dormant under the responsibilities of wife, mother and business owner. Hibernating. But it was always on my mind. It was always in the room. It would come up in conversation with old friends: "Will you make any more music?"

"No time for that," I responded with a smile as my heart ached. Or I'd stub my toe on a box of old CDs in the basement, tears coming to my eyes for more than one reason. My dream of making music for a living hung in the air. Always. It never faded. And I grieved the loss of it. It was an open wound no matter how I tried to heal it. The sadness was ever-present in me. I developed depression and was physically sick most of the time. I was so unhappy. But I didn't make the connection right away. I was in a difficult marriage and didn't have to look far for possible sources of my unhappiness.

Then I had a serious health scare. I had a routine surgery that went wrong, and I bled out. That was a turning point for me. When I was recovering, I made a bucket list. I knew I had to make changes in my life because I did not want to live the way I was living anymore. Bringing music back into my life was at the top of that list. And so I did.

I started playing the piano again. I took songwriting classes. I started going to Nashville to figure out the business of songwriting and learn from the best writers. To become a better writer. I started co-writing and built a network of writers and music friends. I studied publishing, and I founded a record label to start releasing my own music: Willow Sound Records. I studied the business of music. I was slowly waking up. I felt alive. I was finding myself again.

In this new season of my relationship with music, the purpose of making music in my life changed. It was not about making money or "making it," becoming a star or anything like that. I had a much deeper understanding. Music is just part of me. It is woven into the fabric of who I am, like my freckles. I cannot separate "me" from "music." My need to create music was no longer about justifying it or finding my worth in a hit song. I need to make music like I need to breathe. I need to be around music creators because they understand. I need to be helpful to others through music. That is my purpose. Whether I am singing, writing or coaching other artists, music is not something I do. It is who I am.

Being helpful to others in music is the reason for this book. Even if only one thing I've learned along the way can help someone feel more at peace with this mystery that lives inside them called music, then I am honoring my gift.

My hope is that some of my thoughts will resonate with you and this book is helpful to you in some way.

Why listen to me? I say don't. Listen to you. Listen to the resonance within you as you read these words. If it resonates with you, there is truth in it for you. If it doesn't, maybe there will be some helpful practical tips that you can take with you. Either way, know that my words come from my heart and from my experience as a successful entrepreneur, but most importantly, from my deep love for music. And for you - people.

CHAPTER 1
INDIE. REDEFINED

Key Takeaway: This chapter covers what it means to be signed and what it means to be indie in today's music industry ecosystem.

It ain't easy being indie. I think Kermit would agree.

> *Lord, it's not easy being indie*
> *It seems you blend in with so many other ordinary things*
> *And people tend to pass you over*
> *Cause you're not standing out like flashes, sparkles on the water*
> *Or stars in the sky*

It seems being green and being indie have a lot in common. Joe Raposo may have written an anthem Ray Charles can sing for us all!

The journey of an independent artist is not an easy one. It can feel very lonely at times. It takes a toll on the heart and mind. You need constant dedication and commitment to the path. And it can wear you down. Choosing a life and career in music can feel like an endless quest with so many perils. But it can also be magical. It's ups and downs. Highs and lows. This path is no joke. It's not for the faint of heart. Your passion for music needs to burn so bright that it keeps lighting the way because it can feel very dark at times. When it all feels completely overwhelming, naturally, we search for relief. For artists, the hope of relief often comes from the idea of being "signed." Getting signed to a label or publishing company can feel like a great relief…a rescue of sorts. Help finally arriving.

Words are very powerful. In the music industry, the word "signed" has become a powerful word. And more importantly, a definer.

"Signed" has become synonymous with "worthy" or "chosen," sending the message that someone with power will pluck you from the masses, determine you "more special" than others and will now elevate you to stardom. From the outside looking in, it seems that once you are "signed," your problems are solved. You have been discovered, your money problems will disappear and you're going to be famous. All because you got signed. That is one powerful word!

And so we, as music creators, often think we should chase being signed. It becomes not just a goal, but THE goal. Because as humans, it feels good to be "worthy;" it feels really good to be "chosen"- it's the ultimate validation. We are also conditioned to believe that we only have the opportunity to connect our music with a larger audience if and when we are "signed."

But when you look more closely, it becomes clear that being signed doesn't always lead to the promised land. Story upon story of signed artists being shelved, dropped, and worse, ripped off, ending up penniless with no control or access to the music or money they helped create. They are left bitter and disillusioned. And when these artists are cast back into the sea of seekers, it ripples out, carrying a tide of anger fueling the reputation that the music industry is brutal and unfair.

I think there are brutal and unfair people inside the industry, yes. But the business itself is not brutal and unfair; it's really just business. Business is simply about selling a product or service to consumers willing to pay for it. There are business practices that can be unfair, but the essence of business itself is not. It's really about connection. Connecting something(s) to someone(s). However, I do see an inherent problem in the music business that leads to the intense emotions and opinions about the industry. With the music business, the product being sold is ultimately a human being - the artist. Their thoughts and feelings through their songs. Ultimately, what's being marketed and sold is the heart and soul of a human being. Their essence.

If a business makes shoes, a shoe doesn't wrestle with its sense of self or sense of purpose or get addicted to drugs or go through a divorce or have a family. It's just a shoe. Inanimate. Static. It costs x to make, and when you sell it for y, you make z. It's just math.

But artists are human beings. We are not static. We are always in the motion of discovery. Growing and flowing. We are fluid. And a business model that treats human beings as inanimate is bound to cause conflict. Business in its essence is about money, so there still has to be projections and cash-flows and math. And when the math says "shelf the record," "drop the artist," "cancel the tour," although it may solve a math or profit problem, it is someone's life being affected - their self identity, their hopes, their dreams, their families. The fallout from that math equation is broken hearts.

This is not about bashing record labels. Business is business. Major labels are big business. They can be great partners when the time is right. But if an artist signs too early without a full understanding of the nature of that business, it makes them vulnerable. And if they are signing because it fills an emotional need to feel seen, or they want to be saved from their situation, getting signed might feel really good. It'll bring momentary relief and validation. It's a very effective emotional band-aid. In the moment, they'll feel validated, worthy and excited about the possibilities and may not realize it's in fact an emotional band-aid. And it might be too late to realize that they've given their power away in search of relief. The band-aid will eventually fall off.

Big corporations like major labels are beholden to their shareholders and investors. The numbers have to work. Decisions are made to protect the money, not the people. And that can sound harsh. But if you were investing your own hard earned money, millions of dollars, you would want every protection too. The record business is about creativity, but it's also about risk management. And major labels are risk averse for very good financial reasons.

If a business invests millions in red sweaters, and red sweaters sell really, really well, they want to keep selling red sweaters. If you are a yellow sweater, they might like you and think you're great, but investing millions in you when they already know red ones sell is taking risk. History is full of examples of labels taking risks on artists who went on to become huge successes. Big risk, big reward; no risk, no reward. But it is still a risk. There is no predicting what a label may or may not decide. You are the product, not so much a person inside that business model, and that can feel pretty awful at times. But understanding a label's perspective is critical when thinking about doing business with them. And compared to the number of artists signed, the percentage of success stories is very low. It's a long shot in every way. Often, it's a small number of artists on a label financially carrying the entire roster.

And so, if chasing being signed is not the best first move, what is? Getting out there and selling a whole bunch of yellow sweaters on your own first. That way, if and when you're invited to the table to negotiate because you've shown that lots of people want yellow sweaters, you can say, "Hey, I've already sold millions of yellow sweaters, clearly there is a market. You in or out?". That's a much better way to start a relationship with a label. And you'll have options - if the deal is not to your liking, you can walk away because you already built something on your own.

More and more labels want to see proven audience engagement through streams, social media numbers and ticket sales before they consider signing and investing. It's up to you to create that and to understand your leverage when and if you create some buzz to attract a label's attention. They are not there to rescue you - if they come knocking, it's because they see the possibility of money. Which is exciting! Just make sure to keep as big of a piece of it as you can. And remember to give yourself what you need as a human being. Because their first concern will always be the financial bottom line. You need to take care of you.

So, if you're not signed, what are you? You're independent.

WHAT DOES IT MEAN TO BE INDEPENDENT?

If you are an independent artist and you sign a record deal, does that make you a dependent artist? Yes, yes it does. Kidding. Sort of.

As an indie artist, you are the CEO of your own enterprise. You are in business for yourself. You call the shots. As a signed artist, you are closer to being an employee. You are beholden to your employer. You are dependent on your employer to make a living. You are given a job, the support to execute the job and you get a pay cheque. As an unsigned independent artist, you are not given a job to do. You are building a business.

The word independent, or indie for short, has meant different things over the years and morphed the way words do…the first time one of my kids said "sick" with a tone of being impressed, I was thoroughly confused. "He's sick? What's wrong with him?" Yes, that's what I said, and I'm admitting it in print. And just the other day, my daughter picked up our puppy and said,"She doesn't have any cake." I said, "She can't eat cake. She's a puppy." My daughter laughed and said, "Butt. Mom, cake means butt." Again, I found myself thoroughly confused.

Words are fluid…they can morph and change over time as we assign new meaning to them. It's usually young people that find a new angle or new use for a word leaving the older generation clueless. And we older people sound like fools trying to understand the "lingo." Okay, that's a word from my generation that my kids would roll their eyes at…and I digress.

INDIE. REDEFINED

Indie, by definition, means music produced independently from commercial record labels or their subsidiaries, a process that may include an autonomous, do-it-yourself approach to recording and publishing. In the early days of recorded music, it was challenging to record music independently, if not impossible. Recording music could only be done in a studio because of the technology required, and it was expensive so not everyone could access it. Your live show was what you focused on to create buzz, and if you were lucky enough to get something going, you might catch the attention of a label and get signed - which used to be the ultimate goal.

As the decades rolled forward, technology changed from analog to digital and ushered in a whole new way to record music. Studios became more accessible and it was now possible to record music without being signed to a label. The music you released as an independent meant "before you were signed" or "as an unsigned act."

The word indie also took on another meaning, sometimes used to describe a sound or genre. The "indie sound" meant outside of the mainstream, something that sounded different than commercial mainstream music. The indie sound was often less polished, less glossy, more gritty, etc., pushing the boundaries of creativity and often on a lower budget, which led to interesting new combinations of sounds - alternatives to what commercial mainstream was producing.

In that, the word indie also became an attitude in a way. For a long time, indie was the stage you were at before you were signed which was conducive to artists waiting their turn to be chosen. There were only so many spots for signed artists and way more creators than open spots on labels, so it led to a collective frustration and pushback often expressing itself as dissatisfaction with what mainstream was touting as "good" music. And so making "indie" music became about taking a stand in some way, an attitude of standing apart, being your own person, a unique creator because mainstream music was often criticized for all sounding the same. And there was good reason for that.

When a sound is proven to sell, of course the labels want to recreate that sound for financial reasons. It's the red sweaters. The investment is less risky when the product is already proven to sell. But music is art, and when you try to box it up and "label" it, staleness sets in, and we crave something new, something different. We want contrast. There have been genius producers over the decades who instinctively felt that. So they sought out talent that they could create something new with, and those collaborations shifted mainstream sound. You can find examples of that shift over and over again through the decades. That combination of producer and artist brought us the "firsts," the trend setters, the definers of new sounds which influenced generations. The same process repeats itself over and over because creating is always on the leading edge. And as creators, we crave the leading edge - giving birth to something new, ever expanding our relationship and understanding of music and audiences.

Today, the way we consume music has completely changed. Streaming is currently the dominant way to experience music. The technology to record music is both accessible and affordable to almost anyone, and so there is a tremendous amount of music being recorded and released right now. The major labels used to act as a filter of sorts, controlling what music reached the commercial marketplace as the gatekeepers, but now, distribution is accessible to everyone through streaming. Most streaming services do not screen the music that is uploaded, relying instead on the algorithms to decide which music people hear and when.

More than ever before, indie artists have the ability to build their own true fan base and make a sustainable living with their music. But the oversaturation of the marketplace makes it more challenging than ever to get your music heard and build some momentum. Your uploaded song is like a drop of water in the ocean. If you are not making waves, you won't be noticed by the algorithms that determine your song's fate.

The music industry is a little like the Wild West right now where anything goes; any new idea is explored and tried....there is not so much an old guard because the old ways of doing things don't work anymore. Every level of the industry is trying new strategies. New trends, new platforms, new digital marketing, new ideas on music promotion spring up almost weekly. The game is all about the attention economy. We are all competing for attention. Stop scrolling. Click here. Subscribe now. It's all about carving out your share of the attention economy in the digital space - trying every strategy possible to get the user to stop scrolling long enough to listen to what you've created and, hopefully, become a fan.

And as an indie, you are not only creating the music. You have to brand, market, distribute, promote, analyze data, build your audience - all of it. And not everyone has the skills to do everything. And not everyone can afford to hire the people who do have the skills. So it's a really tough road. Indie artists are some of the most resilient and driven entrepreneurs I have ever met. A lot of them give up for good reason - it all becomes too much mentally and emotionally - and financially. If that's you, don't be too hard on yourself. You are not alone.

Being indie is something to be proud of....it is indeed an attitude. Not so much rooted in defiance but empowerment. The great "I Can." And if, as an indie, you build something that a major label is attracted to because it makes money, then that's amazing. Getting into a business partnership with a label to help you get to that next level could be fantastic. But understanding the essence of business and your own point of leverage before you make a decision like that is essential for continued success. Always take the time to align your expectations with anyone you partner with.

It comes down to this: build something that is undeniable. Create what is unapologetically you. And if you build it, they will come. Fans…partners…all of them.

ASK YOURSELF

1. Is the idea of being signed attractive to you? Is that an ultimate goal for you? What do you think it will bring you? What is the most attractive part of it for you?

2. Do you resonate with being an indie artist? Do you have what it takes to build a business around your music? Or do you prefer the idea of working for someone who will tell you where to be and what to do?

3. What does success look like for you? When you imagine yourself in a successful music career what does it look like? Small soft seat theater shows? Millions of followers on Spotify? Large stadium tours around the world? Be honest with yourself. And write it down. There is no right answer here. Every answer is valid. What does success truly look like for you and your music? What will bring you a feeling of satisfaction?

CHAPTER 2
THE CREATIVE CYCLE

 Music gives a soul to the universe, wings to the mind, flight to the imagination and life to everything."

~ PLATO

Key Takeaway: Here we cover the frustrations of being a music creator and the power of changing your perspective; the stages of the creative cycle; the three main elements to success and how to start thinking like an entrepreneur to grow your fan base.

The journey of an artist is very emotional. It's our connection to our emotions that help us create what we create, which is awesome. But being highly emotional creatures can wreak havoc. We are often in our "feels." We feel big. Sometimes our big emotions make it difficult to think clearly. To see the clear path ahead of us and logical steps toward a goal. It's easy to lose our way. And frustration can become the dominant state of being.

A common theme in my coaching became really clear over the years. By the time a client found me, they had often been doing the indie artist thing for a while and were significantly frustrated. They'd spent so much time and money trying to figure out the magic formula for success. I kept hearing, "I feel like I'm not getting anywhere," "I feel like I'm not getting ahead," and "I feel like I'm going in circles" more times than I could count - to the point that I was now greeting new clients with "Let me guess....you feel like you're going around and around in circles getting nowhere," and they'd say, "Yeah, how did you know?"

To me the frustration seems rooted in the disconnect between expectation and outcome. "I expect 100 people to be at my next show - only 10 came out." That's very frustrating, not to mention discouraging. Why did you expect 100? Was it just hope? Or did you analyze and break it down based on data? Simply wishing it so doesn't always make it happen.

In addition to constant frustration, there is also this collective expectation that the journey of an artist is linear: a straight line forward that eventually leads to this mysterious place called Making It. But it isn't. It is in fact a circle. You do go around and around doing the same thing over and over again, but you have a strategy and focused intent, and every time you loop that circle, what you create starts reaching more and more people; your music starts creating a ripple effect in the world that gets bigger and bigger with every cycle. In my mind, I see it as the rings of a tree growing outward and expanding with time until the presence of you and your music in the world is like a great big tree. A willow tree for no reason other than it's my favorite tree. So when it feels like you're going around and around in circles, that's not a bad thing. But ask yourself, am I expanding with every cycle, is something new happening, am I seeing new opportunities, am I seeing evidence that I'm reaching new people? Think of it as growing outward instead of moving forward. Expanding. Getting broader and more firmly rooted instead of racing *toward* something.

Changing your perspective on the rhythm of the journey will help manage your frustration. Understanding what audience growth looks and feels like can help you find a sense of peace and confidence. We are so easily triggered into a state of anxiety, feeling like we are falling behind. But there is no falling behind. Behind who? Where's the race? Who are you running against? It's really only ever about you and the relationship with yourself. The connection between your mind and your heart. So the next time you're scrolling on socials and an artist colleague posts that they won an award, or they got a tour, or got a cut, etc. and you feel your heart sinking, remember your journey is yours and yours alone. Reach for a better thought. Look for evidence in your own life that you are growing and expanding with your own music too. Reach for something inside of you. Try not to measure yourself against other people. Slow and steady, grow those roots deep down, and you'll be able to weather anything.

CREATE. CAPTURE. CONNECT

CREATE

The first step of the cycle is creating - you feel inspired to create music in some form: writing a song, creating a riff, building a beat track, etc. The creative process is the inspiration part, the part where you feel connected to something bigger than yourself, the pull that comes from elsewhere, the melodies that keep you up at night, the beat you drum on the table with your thumb and the lyric that rolls around in your head. The part of you that makes you a music creator. It's when you bring something into the world that was not here before - a piece you play, a song you sing or a track you create in your digital audio workspace. The create stage is where something new is born through you.

CAPTURE

Now you need to take that creation and capture it in a way that allows you to communicate it with others. In my mind, there are two categories of expression here - the performing arts and the recording arts. These art forms are very different, and understanding each of these disciplines is important for success.

When you take something you've created and perform it in your kitchen for your mom, or you busk on a street corner for strangers or on a stage for an audience, you are capturing and communicating your creations as a performer in the performing arts. When you take that creation and make a voice memo on your phone, record a version of it in your home studio or produce a professional recording in a commercial studio, you are capturing and communicating it using the recording arts.

An important difference to note about performing vs. recording is how we communicate as humans. According to a widely referenced study by Albert Mehrabian, when we communicate in person, when there is a visual connection and therefore nonverbal cues, only 7% of that communication is carried by the words alone. The other 93% is nonverbal - 55% body language and 38% tone of voice. So what? Why am I jabbering on about this? So everything.

When you perform a live show, the audience benefits from the nonverbal cues - your body language. The meaning of your lyrics and the essence of the songs you are performing are all being supported by nonverbal communication. Really great artists and entertainers know how to use all elements of communication in their live show. They understand the psychological relationship between the performer and the audience and how to use their authority on stage to bring the audience on a journey. Nonverbal cues are a huge part of this art form. Live music, when it's done well, has this incredible ability to keep us entertained, temporarily distracting us from the worries in our lives but also inspiring us through artistry; it encourages us to be better, to do better. A really great show will leave us changed in some way. And a really great show happens when the performer understands that their entire show should have the rhythm and motion of a conversation with the audience. The whole show is a story being told. A feeling of back and forth energy exchange. Flow. Give and take. A collaborative effort in the expression of you and the receiving of you. Storyteller and listener.

There are many great teachers of this craft, but my go to is Tom Jackson and his Live Music Method. Tom does a great job breaking down how your body language and sense of authority on stage affects the audience and how creating moments in your show is the most important aspect, because all we ever really remember as audience members is how we *felt* during a show. And the moments when we felt it. And then we buy the merch so we can feel that way again. We stream the music to remember that feeling and buy tickets to a next show to relive the feeling of it.

Studio recordings, on the other hand, rely on the auditory senses alone - no visual. So the lyrics, melody and phrasing have to carry all the weight of communicating the essence, emotion and storytelling of your song. The recording process will expose weaknesses in the writing that might be masked by a great live performer. I'll often see artists decide to record a song that they feel has a great audience reaction when they perform it live. But when they release the recorded version, they don't get the reaction they were expecting, and it falls flat. It could be because of the production or arrangement or budget, but it's often due to weaknesses in the writing itself. Once the element of nonverbal communication is removed, the lyric/melody/phrasing are not tight enough to do the job on their own.

Phrasing is the element of the craft that plays the role of nonverbal communication in recorded music. Lining up the important lyric with the strong beats of the bar helps the listener's brain register what you are saying much more clearly. There is so much more to this element of the craft of songwriting, too much to include here, but I highly recommend you explore the teachings of Pat Pattison, a songwriting professor at Berkeley School of Music, to learn more about how important and effective phrasing is and how it contributes to recorded music. I also highly recommend "Song Building: Mastering Lyric Writing" by Marty Dodson, a wonderful songwriter mentor to me.

The important thing to remember is that performing your songs live and recording them for release are two different art forms. They each have their own approach and effective strategies. They are separate crafts. They both help you capture what you create and help you connect it with someone outside yourself, so people can experience what you felt when you were inspired to create it - but they do it in very different ways.

CONNECT

So now you have a live show ready to go and/or a recording ready to release, and it's time to connect it with the world! No matter whether that'll be just in your kitchen singing for your mom, a tour across the country, releasing a single to commercial radio or distributing a full length album, you are connecting your creation with "others" in some way. The connect phase is where you work your promotion, your digital content strategy, radio and streaming campaigns or how you get your mom to come into the kitchen so you can play for her. "Mom! Come here for a sec!" That's not really that different from "Hey! Come to my show!" Or "Hey! Buy my record." It's probably going to be easier to get your mom to the kitchen though - as a mom myself, I'm always beaming with pride when my kids want to show me something they made. Strangers are a little tougher to win over.

And connection is the reason we create at all. First, the connection to our higher selves in the channeling of this magical thing called music and then connection to others so that we can share in the feeling of it all. Connection is everything. It's our why.

AROUND AND AROUND YOU GO

Create. Capture. Connect - over and over again. That's the cycle. And the stages often overlap. You're on tour promoting an album (connect) - and writing for your next album in the van (create). You're in the studio recording (capture) and between takes you're posting on socials to get people out to your next show (connect). It's constant cycling and a lot of juggling. Staying focused is key.

Each part of the cycle has its yin and yang. Creating in the beginning can be really easy, flowing through you effortlessly. As you grow into your career, creating on demand under pressure or deadlines can become stressful.

Carefully curating a live show and performing it for a receptive audience can be intoxicating. Playing the same show on a 50-date tour can be grueling.

Making a record can be an amazing experience. Losing your sense of artistic direction and wrestling with fear of relevancy can make it less pleasant.

Connecting with fans when they love your music feeds the soul. Scrolling through negative comments on socials when they don't can be soul crushing.

There is duality in everything. Being able to ride the ups and downs and maintain your connection to self through it all is the challenge. And also the key to living your best life! Remember, you get to *make music*. How amazing is that?? Soak it up! Every chance you get. What a gift indeed.

GROWING YOUR FAN BASE

So around and around you go, the goal being to expand your presence and grow your reach with every creative cycle.

When you first start out, you will likely rely on your "warm circle," a marketing term that refers to the people in your life connected to you, the human being. These are the people in your world who love you, the person. And as an extension of that, they love what you create. They are the ones at your first show, the ones who buy your first record. They are an incredibly important part of the creator's journey. The hardest part of developing a career as an artist is growing beyond your warm circle. I see many artists who play in only one market over and over, mostly because they can't afford to be out on the road, and they expect the same group of 30 or 40 people - their warm circle - to always come out to their shows. But inevitably, they see their numbers dwindling over time because it's very easy to exhaust your warm circle. They want to support you, but they just can't be the only ones carrying the load for a long period of time. I see a lot of artists giving up at that point with the misguided notion that "if my own family and friends won't come to a show anymore, I must not be very good." But it's not about that. You might be fantastic. But to build a sustainable career, you have to turn some of that warm circle into actual fans and then grow beyond that warm circle.

Not everyone connected to you personally will become a fan, and that's ok! It's not because they don't love you or support you but simply because of musical tastes. Take a group of 40 people - your warm circle. Let's say 32 of them are regular music consumers (it always blows my mind that not everyone listens to music but it's true - a report on www.statista.com shows that almost 20% of people don't listen to music! Blasphemy.) So we take that group of 40 people and reduce it by 20%, which gives us 32 remaining. Now, let's say the genre of music you make is heavy metal. The likelihood that all 32 of those people listen to heavy metal music on a regular basis is pretty low. Let's guess that about one third does. That brings us down to about 10 people out of that original 40 who might have the penchant for your kind of music. How many of those can you turn into actual fans of the way *you* do heavy metal music? That's your realistic goal. If you manage to convert 10 people out of your warm circle of 40, you've done an amazing job. And those 10 will come to everything, every time. And now the trick is going out there in the world and finding 10 more and then 10 more, and 10 more, etc. Before you know it, you have 1000 true fans spending money on the experience of you and your music.

To keep growing and building a career, true fans are essential. Fans are people who come to know you first through your music and then feel connected to you as a person. Hopefully in a healthy way and not in a stan kind of way. A fan's first point of contact with you is your music and then they learn more about you, the person. As opposed to your warm circle, in which they are connected to you as a person first and then come to know your music. Maybe they like your music, maybe they don't, but they'll support you. But fans come to you because they like your music. And nurturing a relationship with them from that point forward is up to you, the artist. Being authentic and consistently committed to building those relationships is the way to create a lasting, loyal fan base.

Fans are everything. Say it out loud with me: Fans. Are. Everything. They power this whole system we call the music industry. Fans are the fuel that keeps the machine churning. And if you create music that makes people feel something, capture it in an interesting way, connect it with an engaged audience and keep nurturing your relationship with your fans, you will keep growing. No doubt. And your ripple effect on the world will keep expanding. If you stay in alignment, stay consistent and commit with long term focused intent, you can grow into a great big willow tree that stands the test of time and sees generations of fans finding shelter in the canopy of your creations.

THE THREE ELEMENTS

I see three essential elements that drive this creative cycle much like water, soil and sun for an actual tree (okay, okay, I love trees. Clearly you have recognized that by now, and it's also why I named my record label after a tree. Trees are awesome). So what are these three elements that propel the growth in you as an artist? Talent, money and drive.

TALENT: this is a somewhat subjective term in the sense that one person may think you're talented and another may not. The only thing that truly matters is whether you believe you have talent. Ed Sheeran is a fantastic example of this. He is a walking masterclass on believing in yourself. In Ed Sheeran's documentary, "Songwriter," he talks about how songwriting is like turning on a tap for the first time. Mostly sludge, mud and dirty water comes out. But when you keep the tap running, eventually crystal clear water is always at the ready. You gotta get the mud out first. And he knew. He just believed that if he stuck with it, because he loved it, he would get somewhere. And not only was he right, he became a force affecting the industry in a major way. If you see videos of him at an early age singing off tune and out of time, you may have been someone who told him that he didn't have what it takes. Ha.

What matters most is what you believe about your talent. So never give your power away to someone who says you're not good enough. Only you know what you're capable of. That being said, learning how to take in external criticism and measure it against what you know to be true inside of yourself is a very useful skill. We need feedback from the people around us to help shape us. But that's not the same as giving your power away - as letting someone else decide what you can and cannot do in this lifetime.

Talent is this unspoken thing that starts with impression and creates connection. It generates a feeling of respect, a feeling of "wow." We often hear grumbling about big labels releasing records on artists that may not be the most "talented," but they have a big machine and big money promotion sending the message that the artist is a star. So you sometimes find yourself sort of agreeing and feeling confused because, if the artist is on every billboard and has multiple hit songs, they must be?

To me, talent is not measured by awards, charts, billboards or sales numbers. Those accolades are a testament to the artist and their team for sure - it takes a lot of hard work to reap those kinds of rewards. But talent is the ability to capture your creation and connect it with others in a way that evokes a memorable emotional reaction. That's it. It doesn't need pizzazz. Pure talent doesn't need smoke and mirrors or fancy billboards.

As an indie artist, resources are likely less abundant, so you need talent to be sustainable. You have to have the ability to create in your own unique and engaging way and be memorable, because there won't be giant billboards reminding people about you. Talent is a special thing. Sometimes it's buried a little and needs some refining. And there are different schools of thought out there…some people believe you can't infuse talent - you either have it or you don't. Others believe you can. Either way, when you witness talent, it's magical and hard to capture with words. It's something that you just feel. It stops you in your tracks. Gets your attention. Makes the room go quiet. It's intangible and undeniable when you witness it. So ask yourself, do you have talent? And how does your talent measure up with what's competing out there? What are you most talented at? And where does your passion lie?

MONEY: this is the greatest source of frustration for most music creators. It is for almost every client I see. There never seems to be enough money. Ever. There's no escaping the fact that it costs money to create/capture/connect your music with the world. Money is an important part of the process, for sure, and learning how to source it and how to manage it is also vital to your success. Later on I'll dive into more specifics about money management, but here, just remember that it's one of the important elements to keep growing. Today more than ever, it's possible to build a career in a sustainable way using a microeconomics approach - it's challenging but definitely more possible than ever because of the internet and advanced recording technology.

An important thing to remember is that if you are truly talented, money will find its way to you. The more talented you are, the less money you need to get some buzz going. People talk, and if they are talking about you, fans will come. People will show interest and offer support because they see it in you, they feel it from you and they want to be a part of it. There is always a way to make it work with whatever budget you have. But you may need to adjust your expectations. If you expect to embark on a global stadium tour right out of the gate and you're frustrated that you can't afford it, you might need to realign your expectations.

DRIVE: To me, this is the absolute most important element. Drive is that internal motivator, that little engine inside yourself that keeps you moving forward. It's what gives birth to your vision and the ambition to realize it. Drive is the one thing you cannot be without. It's the sun. The soil can be lacking and water can be limited, but without the sun, nothing grows. You can have all the talent in the world, but if you don't have drive, the world will never know you and your music. You can have all the money in the world, but if you are not motivated to do the work, the money won't work for you.

If you have drive, you can have less talent and less money and still get something going. Because you believe. And when you believe, all things are possible. Drive is the most important part of the equation, and just like an engine, it needs fuel. Believing in yourself is the fuel that drives you. And only you can generate it. No one can do it for you. You can surround yourself with good people who shore you up when you're feeling low, but ultimately it has to come from inside of you.

When I work with clients, I explain that my job as a coach is to be the GPS. The artist is the engine and the driver. Together we plug in where you want to go, and it's my job to help you get there. I say, "Turn right, turn left, oops U-turn," until you get to your chosen destination. Sometimes, I am also the cruise control, helping to keep the speed steady while we travel, making it a little less tiring. But the artist is always the power behind the wheel. They must be the driver, or it does not work.

IT'S ELEMENTAL DEAR WATSON!

It sums up to this: **a driven, talented artist is bankable**. I guarantee if that's the case for you, and you want to build a team, someone will spend time on you and/or invest money in you. Do the work so you're ready when that time comes, and then you can form true partnerships to help you move to your next level.

MAKING IT YOUR BUSINESS

People make music for all kinds of reasons. A fun hobby, a reason to get together with friends to jam, a side hustle, etc....and it's all valid. Making music, no matter what your reason, is awesome. And jamming with your friends is just as valid and important as playing an arena show. The difference is business.

When you decide that you want to make an income with your music, you are then in business. You are providing a product (songs, albums, merch) and/or a service (live shows) and trading that for money. Aka business. And there are many levels of business.

Let's just say for a minute that your skill is carpentry, not music. You love to create and build with wood. You might just do it as a hobby, building furniture pieces in a shed in your backyard for pure enjoyment. You might give some pieces to friends or family as a gift. You might set up shop and do kitchen cabinetry for local customers. You might move to a bigger shop and hire employees to increase your output and sell your pieces to a larger market. You might get into a partnership with a huge distributor like Amazon and connect your work with people all over the place. If you so choose. Any and all stages are valid. They all matter. It comes down to your life choices. What is your vision for your life? One is not less than the other. It's about preference and lifestyle choices.

There's a natural progression that's easy to see and understand when it comes to skills like carpentry. And if your work is really great, when you tell your friends that you're going to start selling your stuff, they will likely be thrilled for you. They will say things like "It'll be so great if this takes off and it becomes your full time thing because you love it." When you move from your backyard wood shed to a shop in town, they will come to the grand opening and celebrate your success with you.

For some reason, once you announce that you want to make music for a living, it is more often met with skepticism, doubt or reluctance than it is with celebration. Sentiments like " Ok, great. But what's your plan B?", "What's your backup plan?", "Music isn't a real job", "You're just chasing fame" and on and on. You will likely hear these sentiments being expressed in one form or another. There seems to be a common underlying belief that pursuing a career in music and making it a business for yourself is not realistic. It's only a temporary pursuit that will end in failure once you decide to grow up and join the adulting world. I find that so sad. But I see it all the time. Young people coming in for coaching, knowing in their hearts that they truly love music, and the vision for their life is finding a way to make music for a living. But mom and dad want them to go to school to get a degree "just in case." Even if the child has no idea what to study, has no desire to study in that way and will be miserable in that scenario.

I am a mother, so I understand wanting your child to be safe and secure and, most importantly, be able to get a job so they don't live with you for the rest of their lives. But, forcing your child to go to post-secondary school when they don't want to is not about the child. It's about the parent needing to feel good about their parenting. Needing to feel that their child is following the "right" path. A path that is accepted and celebrated by society. Only that path is all about what gives the parent a sense of safety or satisfaction. It's not about the child at all. I see so many clients that come to me as older adults that have experienced something similar, and now that they have done the "responsible" thing, they have time and resources to put toward their music. They are still searching for their joy, which was always in music.

Pursuing music as a career is incredibly brave. You need to be tough, driven, smart, creative and multi-talented to make a go of it. If my child was passionate about music in that way, that would be a beautiful thing. Is it scary? Yes. Because as parents we want our kids to have an easier road than we did. We don't want to see them struggle. But struggle is so, so important. Failure is so important. It shapes us, defines our character and helps us grow in empathy as human beings. We should want that for our kids. Watching them face a challenge so they can see what they're made of...and being there with them for every step. The highs and the lows. I wish more parents celebrated when their kids had a passion for music and supported their efforts to make a living with it. But I will add that as parents, we also know our children. Pursuing music because they have a deep passion for it that is consistent and steady versus pursuing music because they want to be famous are two very different things.

If the attraction to a life in music is for the paparazzi and the fame, that has a very different vibe about it. That path looks very different than the path of creating a life for yourself because you love to make art, you have something to say and you desire connection with others through that expression. If fame comes as a result - great. You'll have an easier time paying your bills. If fame doesn't come, no matter. Because you're motivated by something else. You're motivated by your inner desires. Your passion. And whether you are performing for 50 people or 50,000, your connection to self and your art is the same.

So when and if you do choose to turn your passion into making a living with music, know that the road is challenging but very rewarding. And most importantly, understand that you are now in business. Learning the fundamentals of business will help you achieve success.

ASK YOURSELF

1. When do you feel frustrated? How can you change your perspective?

2. Where are you at in your development in each stage of the creative cycle? Where do you feel you need more support and guidance?

3. Do you have a warm circle? How big is it? How many of them are truly fans? Have you seen any growth beyond that warm circle?

4. How do you feel about the three elements - talent, money & drive? Where do you feel you excel? Where do you feel you are lacking?

5. If you decide to make music your business, what level of business is attractive to you? What resonates with you? Simple and easygoing? Or fast-paced and competitive?

CHAPTER 3
THE CORE PRINCIPLES OF BUSINESS

> *Don't sit down and wait for the opportunities to come. Get up and make them."*
>
> ~ MADAM C.J. WALKER

Key Takeaway: In this chapter we cover how being an everyday consumer provides incredible insight to business; keeping your common sense when it comes to a business in music; how to know if being in the business of music is a good fit for you; how the key to understanding business is understanding yourself as a person.

No matter what level of business most appeals to you, the core principles are the same. The moment you exchange what you create for money from someone or somewhere, you are in business. You're an entrepreneur - a French word that literally means "middle taker" - you facilitated a trade. You stood between the giving of your art and the receiving of money as a trade. How much trading you want to do is up to you. Every level of business is worthy and admirable. It's about what kind of life you want to live. Some music creators love the idea of touring solo in a van playing small shows here and there. That's a beautiful life to them. Some creators want to tour on a tour bus with a whole band, playing 500 cap theaters. That's a beautiful life to them. In either scenario, you are in business.

The music industry itself is exactly that - business. The more you understand how business works, the more easily you can navigate trying to build your business as a music creator. You might think you know nothing about business, and the very thought of it freaks you out. You may even have an adverse reaction to the word business, thinking it's cold and corporate. Or you might love the challenge of it all and think you're a total biz wiz, which would be awesome because you are! The plain truth is, if you are a consumer - if you buy food, clothing, coffee, anything at all - you understand business. If you earn money in some way and you spend that money to survive - you understand business. You may not realize it yet, but you do.

When you go to the grocery store and you're paying attention, you know when you're paying too much for say...lettuce. You might also know the reasons...supply shortage, season, etc. And you may choose to buy it anyway, but you'll have that sense that you're paying a higher price to access it. Equally, you'll know when you're getting a smoking deal on potato chips - three bags for three dollars! I mean come on - sign me up. As consumers, we have an innate sense of the daily cost of living. We may not always understand every nuance, but we understand our own sense of tolerance for what we will pay and what value it brings to us.

As consumers, we understand the concept of value. We instinctively know what we are willing to pay for something. Sometimes it's the limits of our pay cheque that determines what we are willing to pay, and sometimes it's our personal value system. If high-end clothing is important to me because I need it for my job as, let's say a lawyer, because my fees are expensive, I should look expensive to inspire confidence in my services, so I might value the need for high-end clothing. Maybe I want high-end clothing because of the social status attached to it. In that case, maybe I value how people see me and my place in a classist society. If I want good quality but don't really care about the brand name, then I value things that last. Getting the most bang for my buck. If I value getting a deal, I might love thrift shopping. The point being that, as a consumer, we have a sense of what we are comfortable paying and why, which is largely driven by a sense of our values.

If you were to get into the business of a vegetable stand, it's fairly easy to determine the path to success. Find a way to source or grow your vegetables, take that cost, mark it up a bit (that's called margin), keep the pricing competitive and voila! You're in business. Telling people where to find your veggies (promotion) and getting them to believe they should choose your vegetables instead of someone else's (marketing) is the next step. Whether you set up a roadside stand or visit your local grocer to get some space on their shelf, it's easy to describe the steps to success. There is no sense of mystery. It's pretty clear. Everyone needs veggies, you just need to source or grow what your target customer wants, make it affordable and accessible and then get the word out. Easy peasy.

But, for some reason, when it comes to making music, that sense of clarity gets blurred. It's not as clear of a path to success. We can't see the steps to success as easily; there are more variables, and sometimes even our sense of values can get skewed. When you're starting out as an artist, it's a world you might not completely understand. One that is clouded by the "what ifs" that can sneak up on us and confuse our judgement. Sometimes our common sense goes right out the window because of the unknown. I'm gonna spend X on an album, even though I can't afford it because "what if" I'm discovered? "What if" the album is my "big break?" So many times I see clients who have spent more money than they can afford to make records. It's not logical, and I'm always fascinated by what drove them to make those decisions. I've seen clients take out second mortgages on their homes because a random producer told them they could get them a record deal. I've seen couples come to the edge of divorce because savings were spent without discussion. When it comes to trying to "make it" in music, people do crazy things. All in the name of following your dreams. I like dreams. I'm not against following your dreams. But following your heart with your feet on the ground is different than following a dream with your head in the clouds.

There is a driving force in us as music creators - we need to create. It's an intrinsic part of who we are, and it drives us to create. Sometimes, other driving forces are at play, like the need to be validated by others or the need to be discovered and become famous. Choices that are made from that place, that place of filling an emptiness inside us, can throw us off balance because those very strong emotional needs can override logic. It happens when we look outside ourselves for our sense of worth. And that's when you give your power away. You are never going to find a true sense of worth by reaching for something outside yourself. It can only ever come from within and your connection to self. But the big money music business cultivates a culture that reinforces the messaging of being discovered. Being made worthy by that discovery. To maintain a sense of well being and wholeness, you need to be able to identify your own emotional triggers and motivations so that you are less vulnerable to that messaging. Because remember, it's just business. It does not *define* who you are, it's simply an opportunity to *be* who you are.

Let's build a business together for a second. Let's say you want to sell coffee instead of music. You love coffee, and you want to make a living selling coffee. And let's say you have a little bit of startup money but not much. You can't afford a bricks and mortar spot quite yet. What would be your first steps? Think about it for a second. You would need to source some coffee beans and a way to brew them. Then you would need to tell people about your coffee and then connect with the people who want to buy it. The basics of that business are very simple. You have a natural sense of the steps to do this. If you start imagining the scenario, you could easily think of ways to get some customers, especially if you're passionate about your coffee. It all makes sense to you because the concept is simple, and we interact with this thing we call coffee - and business - every single day.

If someone said to you, "No no no...that's not how you do it!" The best way for you to build your coffee business is to sell your coffee to friends and family or even give it away for free. You just keep doing that over and over again until Starbucks discovers you! Hang in there. Your time will come. Wait to be discovered - this is how you make it in the coffee business. You pay your dues slugging it out, waiting for Starbucks to find you, because Starbucks is the only way to get known, but then when they do, you could make millions!

Would you get swept up in the delusion of waiting for a major corporation to make your coffee shop dream come true? Probably not. You would just get to work at building your thing. And if a bigger company came along and wanted to feature your product, sure! Nothing wrong with that. That's fantastic. But it's not the first step. You don't brew a couple of pots of coffee and go knocking on Starbucks' door. I can't tell you how many artists have said to me they think it's time for a record deal after releasing one song.

Instinctively, you have a sense of how to go about things when it's something you're familiar with; you can see how ridiculous that magical thinking is - it's not very logical and it also enforces the idea that you need to put your own fate in someone else's hands. You know that the only thing Starbucks is going to care about is whether your coffee sells. So if your dream is to be in business with Starbucks, you would first focus on building your business. Selling lots and lots of coffee to prove that your coffee sells.

How do you start? You just start selling coffee. And if your coffee is delicious and affordable - heck, even if it isn't - people will start buying it. People will even pay premium prices for coffee (thank you for that lesson, Starbucks). If you're working hard and you have a focused goal, people will come. And not just family and friends - strangers will have heard about your coffee, and they will come check it out. That's called buzz. Buzz creates a ripple effect that will expand your business, and before you know it, you've got a coffee shop on Main Street with staff and a merch line, and when you go home at night, other people keep the coffee shop open for you.

Because you've built a team. You have employees now. There is enough money coming in from selling coffee to feed a team. You did it. You're in business. And then maybe one day, Starbucks walks through the door and says, "Hey, can we talk?"

Building a music business is no different. You have to build it yourself. Build it, and they will come. "They" being your fans, your team, your partners. But you have to build it first. If you feel frustrated because you're peddling your music and there's no buzz, take a step back. Re-evaluate. Because one thing is for sure, if what you're making makes people feel good, they will want it.

Being in business is tough. It is not for the faint of heart. It's not a job. It's a lifestyle. As an entrepreneur, you think about and work your business 24/7. So you want to make sure whatever you are building makes you happy, because that's a lot of life minutes spent doing that thing…you want to be happy along the way. So the very first questions to ask yourself before you decide to make music your business are: Do I love this? Do I love this enough for it to be my life every day? Do I love this enough to make sacrifices for it to succeed? If your answer is an unwavering yes, you probably have the drive to make it a business.

But if there is any hesitation, music might be a wonderful hobby for you. No different than playing a competitive sport when you have a day job. You can play music on the weekends, record music and even release it into the world. It can be a very satisfying and fun activity that does not have to carry the pressure of making money to pay the bills. It's an expensive hobby, and that can be a source of stress, but if you only spend what you can afford, you can find a life balance that includes music. Make music because you love it. Make a business of it if you can't imagine doing anything else and you're okay with taking financial risk.

Building a business with your music is simple in theory but very, very difficult to execute. It is not an easy road. However, right now in today's music industry, it is more possible than ever to make a living with your music because technology is affordable and accessible, and the internet gives us the ability to access and build a fan base on our own. But it takes a lot of marketing skill and a lot of cash-flow over a long period of time to make it work. And most of all it takes consistency.

Most people start off with all the right intentions and even a solid understanding, but then they simply run out. They run out of time or money or energy. Especially as life changes. You might start out when you're single, and then you get married and have children. Or your day job becomes more and more demanding as you move up the ladder, and then you don't have any energy or time left in a day to work on getting your own music business off the ground. So many things can get in the way because the road to building something up from nothing can be a long one.

When someone decides to "give up on the music dream" and give in to the day job, it is often seen and felt as personal failure. Which is so incredibly unfair. The demands of what it takes to build an audience for your music, which in turn creates sustainable income, are so, so heavy. It can make you crazy. Eventually, you might have to let it go for your own sanity's sake. For your family's sake. And that is not a failure. That is okay. Choosing your wellbeing is never a failure. Choosing peace is not failing. You can find a way to have music in your life without it being your main source of income. And it is just as valuable. Just as important. The music you make matters just as much. Making the jump to a full-time living in music as an independent artist is rare and difficult. If everyone could do it, everyone would be doing it - because a life paying your bills with music is pretty sweet.

There is no shortcut. We are fed this idea that you need to be discovered and yes, I keep putting that word in quotations because truthfully, you are discovered all the time...by music lovers who become new fans. So when I say "discovered," I mean by an industry person, which is also misleading because YOU are an industry person. Not only are you an industry person - you ARE the industry. As a music creator, you are the one element that cannot be removed from the industry. The whole system - agents, managers, labels, publishers, fans - completely relies on YOU. The music creator. Without you, there is no industry. So when we are fed this notion that you can only truly get ahead in your career when you are "discovered" by an "industry" person with influence, is it so misleading. We are sold the Cinderella story when in fact it is so much simpler than that. So much more empowering than that. Just make great music that makes you happy. Become enchanted with taking part in something so mysterious and beautiful. The dance with music. How she flows through you and the discovery of what you bring into the world together. That's the fairytale.

It's your love for the music you're creating that will draw in others who will love it too. And when you love the process, when you let yourself fall in love with creating, everything else falls away. The need to be discovered, the need to be famous, the stress of paying the bills. You will find a way. Just focus on the joy of the process and rediscovering yourself as a creator over and over again. You always have to start with that. Your love for music. From there, if you decide that music is a wonderful hobby for you, then fantastic. What a rewarding and fulfilling pastime to have in your life. If you start from there and then also feel the pull for music to be the way you pay your bills, then buckle up. It's a long and bumpy ride. But if you can see it as an adventure, then it's a wonderful journey indeed.

It may seem overly simplistic to compare making your music with selling coffee or opening a vegetable stand, but the core principles really are the same. Make something people want or need, make it well, make it affordable and competitive, make sure people know about what you make, invite them to be part of it and then keep nurturing that customer/fan relationship. It's not rocket science in principle But it is challenging.

In addition to the everyday challenges, I've seen artists struggle with the very idea of being in business. Even the word "business" feels too cold for them. Any talk about making money, marketing yourself, sales, etc. causes them distress. Sometimes it even causes them to feel disdain. It feels inauthentic to them. It's true that the culture around business in our capitalist society has a negative side to it, no doubt. Big corporations prioritize profits over people, leaving destruction in their wake. Major labels are no exception. We have decades of evidence in countless stories of artists being screwed by the music business. And so for some, their instinct is to shy away from any kind of business talk. They are protective of their art - as they should be - and have a mindset that their art will find the right people organically without the need to strategize.

For some, that might be the best approach. For them, discussing strategies and setting goals feels a tad manipulative. Sometimes it even triggers a feeling of "selling out" - creating art solely focused on making money. And that's not a nice feeling. Making music just for money is also not sustainable, because if you are making music that does not feed your own sense of creativity, eventually you will burn out. Over time, it's soul crushing to keep performing music that does not feed your soul. But I do think there is a big difference between making music just to become a rich and famous star and making music that you are passionate about while being deliberate about how you get that music to an audience. Being focused on how to build an audience is not inauthentic or manipulative. It's smart.

Having focused intent because you want to pay your bills with music is not selling out. It's buying in. Buying into the concept that if you excel at your craft, you can and will earn a decent living making music. There is nothing wrong with developing your business skills as an artist. It does not make you less of an artist because you chose to figure out how to make money. Just because you no longer want to be a starving artist or suffer for your art does not make you or your art any less valuable or impactful.

Business is really just about people. Every business provides products and/or services for people. It might not always be in an obvious straight line, but if you follow the line of what a business offers and to whom it sells, eventually it ends with people. Consumers. Understanding people is the trick to being good at business. And the best way to understand people is to understand yourself.

ASK YOURSELF

1. What kind of consumer are you? What motivates you to spend money?

2. Do you find you have a common sense approach to life in general? Do you find you have a common sense approach to getting your music out in the world? Are you influenced by the illusion of the dream?

3. Are you cut out for business? Or does a music hobby feel like a better fit for you? Do you have an entrepreneurial spirit?

CHAPTER 4
BUSINESS IS ABOUT PEOPLE

 You don't build a business - you build people. And then people build the business."

~ ZIG ZIGLAR

Key Takeaway: In this chapter we explore understanding the levels of human need; how important it is to know yourself; how people generally connect with music; your songs are everything; knowing if your music is connecting.

The most important core principle to remember about business is that it is about people. Good news! You are people. So you have everything you need inside of you to understand how business works, and by extension, how to build a business around your music. The magic key is YOU. But understanding yourself as a person requires first, a desire to do so, and second, a lot of courage. It also means you need to be honest with yourself. That can be challenging. Sometimes we don't like what we see. Sometimes we are afraid to discover something about ourselves we prefer not to see. The choice ultimately is yours. The only thing I can tell you for sure is that if you choose to look inward and develop a deeper connection with yourself, you will be much better at business. Not to mention much better at creating your music too.

Study yourself as a person. Look at your life. What are your relationships like? Do you have solid friendships? What's your relationship like with your family? How do you spend your time? Take a minute to look at your schedule. How much time do you spend working? Playing? Downtime? Exercise? All of it. Do some inner work too…how do you feel about yourself as a person? Are you kind? Are you compassionate? Are you a jerk some days? What's your emotional state on most days? Are you calm and peaceful? Are you anxious or depressed? Stop for a few minutes and do an audit of your life. What do you love? What do you not love? What do you want to change? Taking a good look with honesty will not only help you discover yourself in a new way, it will help you see your path in music more clearly.

Notice and reflect on your habits. Study yourself as a consumer. Why did you buy your last pair of shoes? Why did you choose those over another pair? Why did you choose the last restaurant you ate at? Was it the location? Reputation? Availability? Price? Becoming an observer of yourself is the best way to understand people. And in relation to business, discover what motivates you to buy and why. That insight will help you in your business decisions to help build your audience of fans.

Of course, we are not all the same carbon copy of one another, and we make different choices all the time, but at our core, we are motivated by the same things. We are motivated to meet our needs. Human behavior is when we feel a need and desire something that we think will meet that need. We then feel satisfaction when the need is met, and then the next need comes along. Maslow's hierarchy of needs is a really great model for understanding the motivations for human behavior. His theory is widely used as a guide to help understand what we need, when and why.

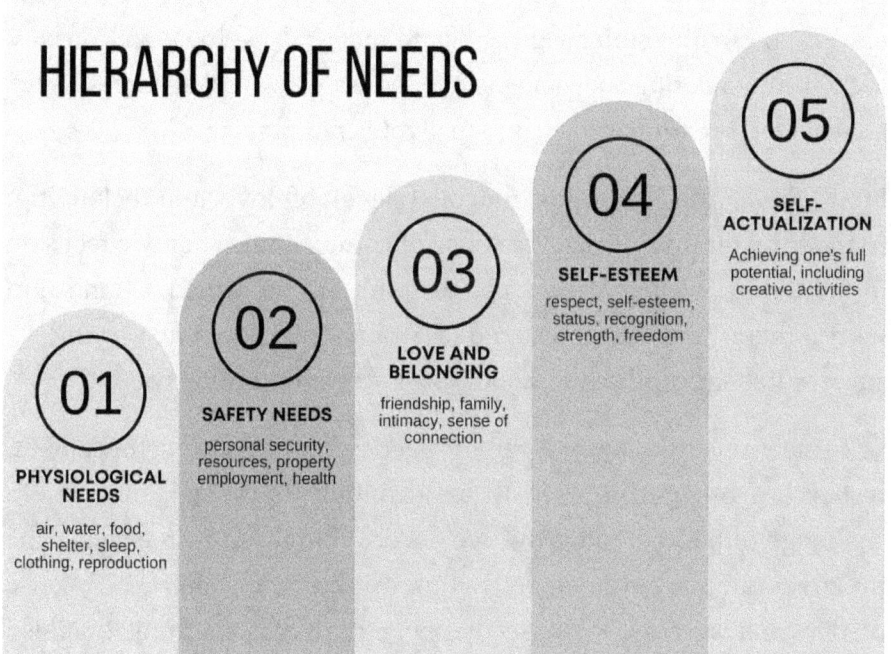

Our basic needs are physiological: breathing, food, water, shelter, clothing, sleep. If these needs are not being met in a consistent, reliable way, we are under stress. We will be constantly distracted and entirely focused on meeting these needs because they are directly related to survival.

If you don't have food or water, writing songs for your next album is not going to be a priority for you. We can't let ourselves be creative when our physiological needs are not being met. Meeting our survival needs will be all-consuming.

The next level of needs according to Maslow's hierarchy is safety and security: health, employment, property, family and social ability. Once we have our physiological needs met, we need a way to continue to acquire them securely. We need a job, so we can buy food. We need access to property so that we have shelter we can rely on. When our physiological needs are met and we have a clear way to continue meeting those needs, we feel safe. We feel secure. We can take a deep breath because our survival is not at risk.

From there, Maslow adds the next level of love and belonging: friendship, family, intimacy, a sense of connection. When we feel safe in the world, we can explore connection with the world. Connection with others. We can then move from head-down-just-trying-to-survive to head-up-having-a look-around beyond ourselves.

Self-esteem is the next level of needs: confidence, achievement, respect for others, the need to be a unique individual. In order to challenge ourselves and grow, we need to build our self-esteem. The understanding of who we are within our societal construct. A sense of personal success. A sense of being part of something but also unique. Having something to offer the world. Feeling understood and seen.

The highest need is self-actualization: morality, creativity, spontaneity, acceptance, purpose, meaning and inner potential. This is where the deepest levels of self discovery happen. This is the day dreaming. The imagining. The uncovering. The full expression of self. The expansion of your being.

If you have food, a place to sleep, clothes on your back, a job, family and friends and you feel good about yourself most of the time, it's easy to be creative. To hear melodies. To write poignant lyrics. But not all of our needs are met all of the time. We flow up and down the hierarchy in different areas of our life. It's fluid. Back and forth. Not a graduated system. Or permanent. You might have regular income coming in and not have to worry about food in your fridge in general. But try sitting down to write a song when you're really hungry. Not gonna happen.

As humans, we have needs. Plain and simple. We also have emotional wounds and trauma. If you are someone who lived with food insecurity as a child, food security as an adult will be important to you. If you've had a romantic partner and they cheat on you, your need for love and belonging will be affected. And possibly tainted until you heal that wound. And there will be some great songs in it too when you move through it. All that to say, your needs and how you meet them are intertwined with your emotional wounds and trauma.

Truly looking at yourself and figuring out why you do what you do and when leads to this amazing, connected place. And the more connected you are with yourself, the more connected you can be with others. Your relationship with yourself sets the tone for every other relationship you have.

Our suffering, our happiness, our pain, our joy…..it's all part of this amazing thing we call life. The human experience. And it's a collective one. Even though we are individuals, we are having a collective experience. Any insight into who you are is also insight into who others might be. So be curious! Take a minute and connect how you feel. What you believe about yourself. And study your habits. Get to know your why. Look at the last thing you purchased. Why did you purchase it? Which of your needs is it meeting? And stay curious. Become a great observer of yourself and others because it's the key to success - as a person and in business. Simple as that.

In your business as a music creator, you are the product. You are selling the experience of you…your songs, your show, your merch, your social media content…it's all the experience of you. Your thoughts, your feelings, what you have to say and what you have to offer the world. The better you know yourself, the better positioned you are to communicate who you are and build an audience that will connect with what you have to offer.

LIPS, HIPS & SKIPS

Although we have much in common in the collective experience of being human and the motivation to meet our needs, how we go about meeting those needs is personal preference. We each have our own personal preferences. And this is so true in music. Not everyone is going to like your music. And that's okay. You will not be everyone's cup of tea. But if you want to make a living with your music, it needs to connect with someone. Preferably a lot of someones. Knowing whether your music connects with an audience is important. Sometimes we are so consumed by the feel good experience of creating, that we don't stop to check in and make sure our music connects.

This is not about whether your music is "good" or "bad" - that's way too subjective. In order for your music to be commercially viable - meaning it will elicit commerce aka sell to a lot of someones - it has to connect on some level. And with music, connecting emotionally is the primary driver. Music can connect intellectually too, but how it makes us feel is what we remember. So how do you know if your music is connecting? Remember this: it's all about lips, hips and skips.

Lips. Does your music make people want to sing along? Do they remember the words?

Hips. Does your music make people want to dance? Does it get them up and moving? Make them want to sway along?

Skips. Does your music make their heart skip a beat? Feel something so deeply it stops them, grabs hold of them?

Everything you create is worthy and matters. But knowing whether your music connects with an audience is where you'll start making money to earn a living. The audience is everything. How they connect with your music is everything. We create so that we can share what we think and feel with others - it's the whole reason we do what we do. Some writers might say they create for themselves, for the process of it. But they still do it because they want to be heard and feel seen. If you aren't so concerned with the business of your music, creating for the process of it is just fine. But when you want to earn a living, your music needs to connect with others. It needs to make them feel something. And then they will buy it to feel that way again.

IT'S ALL ABOUT THE SONG

I think this is the area where I get the most resistance from developing artists and writers. When artists/writers are starting out, they often believe that what they write on the first draft is ready for the world. That the inspiration flowing through them should not be tampered with…that they have channeled precious art into the world. And they have. To a degree. But the mastery of the craft is not in the first draft, the original point of inspiration. The mastery of the craft is in the rewriting. In the digging deep. Stretching and compressing, holding your work up to the light and looking at it from all angles. There are very few, if any, successful writers who record and release music they wrote in one draft. There are exceptions of course. Dolly Parton is an exception. Word is she wrote "I Will Always Love You" & "Jolene" on the same night up in her back bedroom. But there is only one Dolly. And she wrote hundreds and hundreds of songs before that. Could you be a Dolly? Sure. Is it the norm? No.

Learning the craft of songwriting and the process of rewriting is such an important tool. And there are so many amazing songwriting books and coaches out there. I've listed some of my favorites at the back of the book. There is so much to the craft of songwriting that I won't go into all the details here but I can give some helpful tips.

Something I see often with developing artists/writers is confusing lack of connection with lack of preference. If they are not seeing consistent connection with their music or consistent audience growth, they'll end up thinking, "Oh, they just don't get me and my art," that kind of thing. And yes, some people may not prefer your type of music. But if they can't understand it, if it's confusing and doesn't make them feel anything, that's a different issue. Say you write a song about a yellow bird and play it for someone. If their response is, "Nice song about a black cat," there's a disconnect. Something in your lyric caused confusion. This is not lack of preference - this is lack of connection.

If you write a song about a yellow bird and their response is, "Great song about a canary," now you've connected. You, as the writer, might have been picturing a parrot as your yellow bird when you wrote the song, but the listener put their own yellow bird in there. No disconnect. They received the story about the yellow bird, but their imagination conjured up a different kind of yellow bird. They put their own stuff in it. But you and the listener connected on the story about a yellow bird. That's the beauty about songwriting. A well-written song is not confusing. It leaves room for the listener to put their own personal experiences in there. Their own movie in their mind.

Some writers are more poetic than others. Some are literal. There is no right or wrong in songwriting. Just connection. Leonard Cohen comes to mind. His writing is more abstract than a Katy Perry pop song, but you feel it. You connect emotionally. Joni Mitchell too. Some of her lyrics are straight up conversational, and some are more poetic. But you feel her. You feel the meaning. Even if it's not spelled out for you. When songwriters get really good at their craft, they also develop a kind of fingerprint in their writing, a style and a way of saying things that is unique to them. Alanis Morissette has a way of phrasing syllables like no one else. It is unique to her writing style, and you can spot an Alanis song from the first line.

Songs run the gamut of abstract poetry to relaxed, conversational lyric. As you develop your voice and your style in your writing, you'll start to see a pattern too. And so will others. I have a deep love and respect for the craft of songwriting. I spent years learning from some of the best because I wanted to become the best writer I could be. It's a lifelong process of self discovery and partnership with this magical thing called creating. Even when you have a solid understanding of the fundamentals, there is no "there." There is no place of arrival where you have it all figured out all of the time. As a writer, you are always looking for a new way to say the same thing. A unique angle or interesting way to tell the same story that's been told a thousand times.

It's challenging and beautiful and heart-wrenching and satisfying, and it can make you crazy sometimes. And elated other times. If you know, you know. Being a songwriter is a really incredible thing. So when you get frustrated, remember that the gift you have is unique and wonderful. Be gentle with yourself. Most of all, stay open to the mystery of it all. I've had the chance to write with Hall of Fame and Grammy winning writers. There was a common theme. Even though they were writing with an up-and-coming, developing writer, there was never any sense of superiority. There was always common respect in the room. They were just as entranced by the muse as I was, still after all the years and accolades in their careers. It was humbling to witness and a wonderful reminder that, no matter how successful you become as a music creator, you are at the mercy of the channel. Keep your heart and mind open at all times. I heard Rivers Rutherford when accepting his Songwriter Hall of Fame Award describe it in the most beautiful way: "Our job as songwriters is to provide a channel for the story to come through without the static of our ego getting in the way." That stuck. And has stayed with me ever since.

No matter what your approach to songwriting is or how you get there, your songs need to connect. And not just because you think they do in your mind. Look for tangible evidence that your songs make someone feel something. And slow down. Don't be in a rush to record your songs. Try them out on a live audience first to see how they land. Gauge how the song is received. When you perform your songs live and you're tuned in to your audience, you can feel whether the songs connect or not. Listen to the feedback after the show: "I really loved that song about the yellow bird," "What was the name of the song about the yellow bird again?"and "Can I stream that song yet?," that kind of stuff. Pay attention to what your audience is telling you. It's market research. There are clues in all of it. Really listen to what they say. Who is saying it? Your mom doesn't count. Sorry. I'm a mom, and moms are awesome. Moms cannot give objective feedback. Unless they, themselves, are a professional songwriter. Moms will always see you through the love lens. That's their job! They are supposed to be the safe place you go to always feel loved.

That being said, you do need to form a small group of trusted people to give you honest and objective feedback on your songs. When you're starting out, you probably won't have a publisher yet, but when you do have someone acting in that role for you, they will be a wonderful guide for your writing. But at first, you'll have to rely on people you can easily access and people you trust, which usually comes down to family and friends. And this can be a good thing and also a terrible thing.

What will commonly happen is that you'll say to your family or friend, "Hey, I wrote a song. I'll play it for you, so let me know what you think." Don't do it! Don't ask loved ones what they <u>think</u> of your song. If they are not professional songwriters, you don't want to know what they think of your song. That's not helpful at all. They don't have the skill to give you that kind of direction. And the feedback will be undoubtedly tainted by the personal relationship with you as a person. They might hesitate to speak their truth for fear of hurting your feelings or damaging your relationship. It's not nice to set them up like that! And it's a waste of time for you. On the surface, it seems logical to ask people you know what they think of your song because you write songs for people to hear. But asking people what they think while you're still working the song will not help you with your craft. It will more likely cause you some confusion because so-and-so might say they love it and then so-and-so says it's just okay and then someone else says they don't get it. So you're left spinning not knowing which feedback to trust.

This happens with song critique services too. There are some wonderful song critique services out there. And I believe they are all well-meaning. But I see so, so many artists/writers disheartened and confused by the inconsistent feedback they receive. It's very difficult to provide feedback on a song without context or an ongoing relationship with the writer. Context is everything. If someone sends in a song for critique, and in their minds they are writing a song for their grandmother's birthday celebration, but the critique comes back from the standpoint of a Reba McEntire cut, the feedback is going to be way out of alignment. Understanding the purpose of the song from the writer's mind is key to giving feedback that will be actually helpful to them. Finding a songwriting coach is a good way to develop your writing. When a coach gets to know a writer, they develop a sense of their progress, so it's easier to praise areas where they are improving and then give them some direction on other areas to focus on as opposed to a one shot deal.

For you, the writer, it's important to put feedback into perspective. The only feedback that ever really truly matters is from your audience and fans. But until you get your music out there, learning how to take in constructive criticism about your art is a skill. Give it thought but not too much weight. Don't put all your eggs in one critique basket. Take in the comments, see what fits for you and leave the rest. And don't hang on to every word as if it will determine the song's fate. I've had writers reach out for my comments on their songs, which I gave, and if they didn't like what I had to say, they would dismiss it, saying, "Well, so-and-so said my song was a hit." Okay, great! Then don't go to other people for feedback if you're dug in and holding on to that feedback as the holy grail. Keep an open heart, open mind. Keep feedback on your music in perspective. Be curious. Take it in. But don't let it completely define you. And if someone is qualified to comment or coach you on your songwriting, they will be able to back up why they are saying what they are saying - it won't just be their opinion. It'll be about the craft and why something is working or why it's not.

If you're not sending your songs out for critiques or working with a publisher or a coach, then here's an exercise you can use with your friends and family. The most valuable feedback you can get from someone you are testing your songs on is how they are experiencing the song. Before you play them the song, ask them to make note of these things when they listen:

SEEING

Does the song start a movie in their mind? Do they see clear pictures in their head as the story moves along?

FEELING

Does the song make them feel anything? If yes, what emotions come up for them?

CONNECTING

Did they stay connected to the song all the way through? Was there any disconnect? Did they notice their mind wandering? And if so, at which point? Was there anything confusing about the lyric?

That kind of feedback is actually helpful. Using this approach, the friends and family around you can be more effective in helping you with your development. If they don't see a movie in their mind, your lyricism is not telling the story clearly enough. If they don't feel any emotion, it's not yet conveying the feeling you had when you wrote it. If they notice their minds wandering while trying to listen, there's a disconnect. Take in the feedback and go rewrite. Don't settle. Keep working at it until your song connects.

Your most important product in the business of your music is the songs. Hands down. It should always be music first. Everything else is secondary. Make sure your songs connect - they make people move their lips and want to sing along, move their hips to dance or feel their heart skip a beat with the feeling of the story. Now you have something you can build a business on.

Remember, it's always about people. First, understanding yourself as a person - what drives you to do what you do. Then understanding yourself as a creator. Then paying attention to whether your music connects with other people. Understanding yourself to understand consumers and then using that to inform building an audience that wants to consume what you create. Inward, then outward. What you see inside yourself and how it's reflected out in the world. Understand people, and you understand how to be successful in business.

ASK YOURSELF

1. How do you meet your needs? What are your emotional drivers? Do you recognize any emotional wounds or trauma? When do you feel satisfied and content? How well do you know yourself? Do you like what you see?

2. What evidence do you have that your songs are connecting with people? Can your songs compete with what's in the marketplace right now? Does your music make people want to sing, dance or feel their heart skip a beat? Do you have evidence of it?

3. Do you see the link between understanding yourself, understanding people and being successful at building your business?

CHAPTER 5
MONEY, MONEY, MONEY

 All money is a matter of belief."

~ ADAM SMITH

Key Takeaway: In this chapter we cover the importance of your relationship with money; how your beliefs about your own worth are expressed through money; how money is the life blood of every business.

There's a common joke in the music business: If you want to make a million dollars in the music industry, spend two. It's funny because there is truth to it. Making music costs a lot of money, and it's difficult to make that money back. As an indie, you're spending your own money. In a label deal, they provide the cash-flow, but it's your money, and you'll owe that money back. So really, they spend your money for you. Spending your own money comes with risk.

Accessing money, knowing how to manage it properly and knowing how to make money with the money you do have - all of that is business management. Whether you're in a deal or you're independent, paying attention to that business management matters.

In a label deal (I'm over simplifying here because there are many types of label deals), the label fronts the cash for your project, but it's a debt. It's called a recoupable. Not only do you owe that money back to them, they can change the loan amount at any time without your permission. It's like going to a bank and getting a loan for $10,000 and then when you check your statement at a later date, they've increased the amount of the loan to $15,000 without your say-so. It's not a great situation. And the income generated from your music doesn't all go toward paying down your recoupable.

The basic concept is this:

You sign a deal. Let's say your split of the income generated from the music is 10% and the label gets 90%. The label then spends $100,000 on your project. They start selling your albums. You sell your first album for $10 - so $1 goes to you and $9 goes to the label. But you don't actually get your $1. It pays down the recoupable. Now you owe the label $99,999. But they get to keep their $9. I'm going to let you read that again so it sinks in. I'll wait. They keep their $9.

This is not a good business deal for you. You want to cash-flow your projects on your own as much as you possibly can. Again, it's over simplified - the numbers might be different, but the structure of the deal will most definitely benefit the label, not you. They are taking the risk fronting the money for your project, and the reward for that risk is most of the income. They can also add to the $100,000 debt anytime. Let's say they decide you need a $30,000 video - it gets tacked on. And now, because recorded music no longer brings in the same income it used to before streaming, current record deals are now structured as what's called 360s. Meaning the label gets a percentage of all the income you bring in - not just the sale/streams of your music. You give up a percentage of your live show fees, your merchandise sales, your publishing, royalties, writer share, etc. They get a piece of the whole pie, hence the term 360. And all that money goes to them, not to pay down your debt.

Again, not great for you. Staying independent as long as you can is better for you financially. But you do need money to keep making music. It has to come from somewhere.

Most indie artists I work with struggle with money. For all kinds of reasons. They don't have enough of it, mostly. For some clients who have families and other financial responsibilities, it can be difficult to balance how much of the family's money to spend on music. Especially if both partners are not on the same page as far as valuing music. Some other times, the artist has borrowed money from family or friends, and it has caused strain on the relationship.

Money can be a real source of stress. But it can also bring a feeling of freedom when you have a lot of it. Your attitude toward and relationship with money will have a huge impact on your success in making music for a living.

www.Empower.Me has a really fun psychology quiz that I use in my workshops to help clients uncover their own relationship with money. They break it down to six money personalities. See which one resonates most with you:

1. **The Idealist**: You're aware that money is a necessary part of life, but you'd rather not get bogged down with it.

2. **The Stockpiler**: You're always saving for a rainy day, just in case.

3. **The Hedonist**: You know how to enjoy life. Money's not going to get in the way of your freedom!

4. **The Celebrity**: Why settle for the ordinary when you can buy yourself the extraordinary?

5. **The Nurturer**: Your savings provide for the people you love if they ever find themselves in a pinch.

6. **The Conqueror**: Making money comes naturally to you because work is the love of your life.

Notice how you feel about each statement. Notice what your body feels and where you feel it with each statement. Do you feel anxious? Excited? Sad? There will be clues about your beliefs about money in the way you feel about it.

Understanding how you feel about money helps you uncover your motivations around money. I grew up with a sense of food insecurity. The fear that resources were going to run out. So I carried anxiety when it came to food security into my adult life, which created a strong driver. Making sure I always have enough money to meet my own and my family's physiological needs is so strong that sometimes I choose not to spend money on doing something fun "just in case," even when I have the expendable income. As I became more aware of this pattern, I also noticed that I had a habit of leaving one bite of food left on my plate or one sip left in my coffee or drink. And if I tried to finish it, I was hit with a wave of panic. It was my subconscious mind protecting me. Leaving one bite meant there was still food left. I was safe.

Our childhood experiences solidify core beliefs about the world. Subconscious programming drives a lot of our behaviors. Becoming aware of those patterns, particularly in regards to your behavior when it comes to money, will more firmly position you in the driver seat of your life.

Whatever your relationship is with money, whether healthy or unhealthy, it will have a big impact on building a successful business with your music. Look at the patterns in your life. Do you overspend? Do you underspend? Are you in debt? Are you scared of debt? Be aware of the patterns because what you believe about money will express itself in the functioning of your business. Having a handle on how you feel about money will help you make better decisions around what to spend and when. You want to feel good about making music. So you need to feel good about the money you spend on it.

Money is a currency. So is time. We spend our time on the things we value most. We do the same with money. What do you value? Does spending money feel good? When? Does spending money feel bad? When? Are you in a state of flow when it comes to money, or do you feel resistance around it?

There's a "money tree" song that went viral on TikTok. There's something powerful in the rhythm of these words. So if you find yourself feeling resistance around money, the lack of it, the need for more and no idea where it will come from, this might help ease it a bit. I've been known to chant this with my team at the label when we're not sure how we'll make it to the next month. Even if it feels ridiculous to you, it's still fun to recite it.

> *Ching, ching, ching, goes the money tree*
> *Every time I ching money comes to me*
> *It all flows in so abundantly*
> *From the top, left, right and up under me*
> *Wave, wave, wave, I'm a money wave*
> *Money flow, money flow, money made*
> *Flowing in and out plus money saved*
> *Debt, debt, debt, all debt is paid*

So many people resonated with this that it went viral. The struggle with money is not uncommon, clearly. And for indie artists, it's more common than not.

I could spend dozens of chapters telling you where you can source money, how to apply for grants, how to pitch to investors and how to manage your money, but that would be a whole other book in itself. And there are plenty of great books about money out there. What I'm focused on is YOU and your relationship with money. What I know for sure is, your own relationship with money will dictate how much money you are able to find or attract to fund your music business. So the best first step is to dig deep and have an honest look about your thoughts and feelings around money.

HOW YOU FEEL ABOUT YOUR OWN WORTH

"How much should I charge for a gig?" has to be in the top three questions I'm asked constantly. Developing a sense of what your show and your music are worth to the buying public is a process. What I've noticed over the years is that what someone is comfortable charging is inextricably linked to how they feel about their own self-worth. How do you feel about charging for your music? Does it make you uncomfortable? Or is it easy breezy for you to come up with a number? Our own self-worth will influence our view of what we should charge for what we do. That's one layer.

The other layer is economics, what the market will allow. Some areas are easier than others. For streaming rates, the DSPs set the rates. For your hard copy albums and merch, you'll use what other artists charge at their shows as a guide. For licensing, it'll be a negotiation, or the publishers/music supervisors will set the rates. But when it comes to your live show, unless you're signed to a booking agent who will set your rate, you've got to decide for yourself what your show is worth.

The first place to start is what will the show cost you? Make a budget. Venue rental, promotion, marketing, players, sound, lights, videography, etc. Then take the capacity of the venue. Decide on the ticket price. What do artists at your level charge for a show at that venue typically? Do some research. Who has played there before? What is your draw in that market? Take an average of that and then set your ticket price so they are as low as they can be to still make money and communicate the level of quality your show will be.

The economics part is a bit easier because there are not really a lot of emotions that come into it. Maybe some doubt or anxiety around how many people will actually come out, but the rest is really just math.

But when someone wants to hire you to play, setting a fee is the one place where your own sense of self-worth can creep in and influence the process. First thing to do is calculate what it will cost you to provide the entertainment: your players, rehearsal time, rehearsal space, etc. From there, evaluate the event. Is it a wedding? What's the going rate for that service? What have you charged in the past? What's the lowest fee you're willing to do it for? What is the client willing to pay? You take all of these elements and work your way to a fee that is likely to get you the gig. You have to be okay with walking away too. If it comes to that.

Negotiation is a skill that you develop over time. Once you have a handle on all the factors and some experience in quoting, it gets easier. But if your own sense of self-worth is low, you will feel weird or uncomfortable about charging a reasonable fee. You'll feel things like guilt or anxiety. It might feel selfish. It might feel unfair. If you feel strong negative emotions come up when you're trying to quote a fee for your service, take notice of it. Where is it coming from? What do you believe about yourself and your value? Try to separate the economics of it from the emotions.

MONEY IS THE LIFEBLOOD OF EVERY BUSINESS

Money in. Money out. Yep, that's it. The whole thing. The game is to have more money coming in than going out. That's how you stay in business. That's how you grow a business. If you don't learn how money flows in the music business, it'll be the thing that sinks you.

Navigating the financial part of the music business can feel very overwhelming. When I first started out, it felt like there was this mysterious black box with secret information I did not have access to. I had no idea how money was made with music. I heard terms like royalties and licensing and streaming rates but felt quite confused by it all. If that's you, you are not alone. Keep breathing. Here are the basic building blocks of how to make money with your music:

Music Income Streams - What are your products and services? Live shows, merchandise, music masters and songs. For each of these income streams, think about the money in/money out equation.

What are the costs to put on your show? How much do you have to sell your tickets for in order to cover the cost? How many people can you draw?

You make a record - how much will it cost? How many streams and album sales do you need to recover that cost? Do you have enough fans yet who will want to buy?

You create merchandise - how much did it cost to make? How much do you have to sell it for to break even? To make a profit?

DO THE MATH. Don't run your business on a whim or a hope and a prayer that it will all come together. Sit down with a pen, paper and calculator. Do the math. And keep records so you see the growth and the areas you're doing well in and where you need to focus more effort.

Don't be afraid to work the numbers. Don't hide from the truth of it. It's just math. Numbers don't lie, and the numbers will show you what's possible. Make conscious choices about when you're going to take a loss i.e. you want to do a live show in a new city, and you won't draw enough people to cover all your costs, but you'll start a relationship with a new venue and seed the market. Everything is a trade. Instead of thinking about it as losing money on a show, you're investing in a new market. Everything is a mindset. It's about how to look at it. Sometimes it's easier than others. "I can't pay my rent this month," might become, "This is a chance to reconnect with my landlord." Just kidding. Not being able to pay your rent is very stressful. It's not fun at all to live like that. But if you're consistently in that situation, what are the numbers telling you? You need to re-evaluate your living situation. Everything is a choice. And if you don't like the feeling of being stressed about money, make a change to your situation.

If you're in business, there is no escaping dealing with money. You can't run from it. Eventually you will have to face it. Find a way to make friends with the concept of money. Make friends with you. Believe in yourself and your worth. Money is great! You're great! Money is not the root of all evil. It's not wrong to make money. It's not selfish. It's awesome. Money means you get to keep doing what you love to do! Attract that stuff all day long and celebrate the flow of money. Ching, ching, ching goes the money tree…

ASK YOURSELF

1. What's your relationship with money? Which money personality do you have?

2. What is your sense of self worth? Do you believe you bring value? Do you believe you have something to offer? Do you believe it's okay for you to be compensated properly for what you do?

3. Do you track your money well? Do you have a good sense of how your money is flowing? Do you think it's important to know where your money is going and where it's coming from?

CHAPTER 6
LOOK FOR THE HELPERS

 You, an aspiring writer, can get help from teachers, but you are going to have to learn a lot by yourself, sitting alone in a room."

~ DR. SEUSS

Key Takeaway: Hiring someone to help with your artist development makes good sense; the most common roles in the music business; how to spot a scam.

There are many different kinds of helpers you will need along your journey as a music creator. You'll need certain skill sets at different times as you grow your team and move through the levels of your career. Sadly, the music industry has a bad reputation for taking advantage of people, and so finding help you can trust can be tricky. Knowing how to vet someone properly is important. Understanding exactly what you need and what you're looking for is equally important. It used to be somewhat of an unspoken rule in the business that if someone was charging you money to help develop you, it was likely not legit. Industry professionals involved in artist development typically worked on a percentage basis, meaning they got a cut of the work you generated together so you, the artist, didn't have to pay fees out of pocket for their services. So, if someone was asking you to pay fees out of pocket before you really got anything going, it was a red flag.

These days, it's a bit different. There are still people in artist development to watch out for - there are plenty of agencies charging thousands per month to help you "launch your career" or "get you a record deal," but there are a lot of legit industry professionals working in artist development who can actually help you. A good rule of thumb is that anyone making promises or guarantees should probably be avoided. Another good rule of thumb is if you can't afford it, don't do it. If paying high fees for artist development is going to put you in debt, don't do it. There's a better way. Also, you need as much money as possible to create the assets you need to build your business, so if you spend most of your available cash on hiring someone to help you, you won't have enough left over to actually do the things that person says you need to do.

I am an example of someone who works in artist development. I founded a membership community called The (Gro)ve for music creators. We do charge a fee for our time because our focus is empowerment and education. We don't promise to make anyone a star. We offer a coaching service focused on the steps to develop the artist's music, their show and their brand and work with them to build their audience. We consider it a success when a client doesn't need us anymore. When we have packed their saddlebags with the knowledge they need and sent them on their way to work the method, that's a win! And then it frees up a spot for another developing artist to get some coaching. The fees for our service are comparable to taking piano or guitar lessons. But instead of teaching how to play music, we teach about building your business as an artist instead. Even though we are affordable, credible and have a proven working model, we still get questioned sometimes. Because some people still think that if we "believed" in the artist, we would work for free. The sad reality is, we can believe in the artist all day long, but it's gonna take a long time and a lot of cash to get that artist off the ground. The chances of the artist eventually generating enough money to cover all of our time and effort in that pursuit are pretty slim. Especially at the starting levels when audiences are smaller.

In any other industry, when a business needs some guidance to get where they want to go, they hire consultants. It's not unusual or suspicious. It's common practice. It makes good sense to use a consultant or coach to help build your business as an artist. If they are affordable for you and you see results, it's a great way to build your team. It also keeps you owning all of your music without giving up a percentage of your masters or your publishing. Finding a good artist development coach is a great first step when you're ready to start building an audience and treating your music as a business.

Artist development is about guiding, not deciding. If you are working with someone to help you, make sure they don't become the voice that is you. They should be helping you hear your own inner voice. Not replacing it. When someone comes to work with me and says, "I want to be a stadium-selling global super star!" and then they sing for me, making it clear that they are completely tone deaf, my job isn't to say, "You're not good enough" or "You'll never make it." My job is to say, "The first step is singing lessons." My job as a development coach is to help them see the steps to realizing their vision. And sometimes, to help them realize that the vision for their life might not be attainable. I try to make visible what might be invisible to them. Sometimes through the coaching process, it becomes clear that their "why" might be misplaced. That their inner drive comes from a wounded place as opposed to an inspired vision. But the realization has to come from within them, through the process of self-discovery, not from my opinion.

When you're looking for some help and are vetting people, take the time to do your research. Ask for references. Do some digging on who they've worked with before. Ask a lot of questions. Take the time to get a sense of the kind of person they are, their personality, their values. You want to work with people who share your same values. And certainly people you can trust. Don't compromise your values because you think a person can make a difference in your career. It'll come back to bite you. Surround yourself with people you genuinely like and would invite to have a seat at your kitchen table. If something feels "off" about someone, trust your gut. It's okay to be selective about who you bring onto your team. Even when you're just starting out.

There are many, many roles in the industry. But here are a few of the main ones and when you might need them:

I NEED A MANAGER! LIKE, RIGHT NOW.

When you find yourself thinking "I need a manager!!", it's more likely that you are feeling overwhelmed, confused and just need some help to feel better. If your desire to get a manager is coming from that place, you don't really need a manager yet. A development coach would probably suffice. You will need a manager at some point, and you'll know you're there when there's actually stuff that needs to be managed. Not just problems to solve but opportunities that need to be managed. When you can take the money you make from music, set aside 15 - 20% and still make money, then you know you can afford a manager. If no money is coming in, how is your manager going to eat and pay their rent? Finding a manager may help you feel better, but what does it do for them?

When you're looking to add a manager to your team (or anyone for that matter), it's a good idea to ask yourself, "What do I bring to THEM?" Not, "Come help ME make me lots of money and then you can get paid." Remember you're building a business. If you were running a coffee shop, you wouldn't hire a manager and say, "We're not making enough money to pay you right now, but if you do a really great job managing the coffee shop and generate more business, then we can give you a percentage of the income you generate." I think you would be hard pressed to find someone willing to take that risk without being an owner. But you might find friends or family willing to, and that's common in music too. A family member or friend will take on the role of manager in the early days to help an artist get started. That can be great. It can also get sticky. Especially if communication skills aren't great. If expectations aren't properly and honestly communicated, it can lead to bruised feelings in the relationship. Particularly when and if money does start flowing. So if you do work with friends or family at the start, take a minute to write down the job description, the expectation and the compensation - whatever it may be - so that if there's a breakdown in communication, you can always refer back to what you wrote down and agreed to together. It doesn't have to be fancy, and it doesn't have to be a contract. Just a point in time where you write down each of your expectations and understandings of the roles so that you can refer to it later if a problem arises.

Finding the right professional manager is a pretty big deal. It's almost like finding a spouse. The partnership should be that strong, that committed. Because it's a long haul, and you'll ideally be with that person for years to come. Take your time to find the right match, and don't rush. It's an important decision. You want someone to handle the day to day stuff but also have a clear sense of the vision for your career. You want to feel comfortable with them representing you out there in the world. You also want to know that the impression they make while representing you reflects you and your values.

Compensation for managers might be entirely percentage based at around 15-20% of your gross income. It can be a hybrid model, meaning you pay a flat fee per month to cover their time plus a percentage of your gross earnings. Or it could be just a monthly fee with no compensation from your gross income. Whichever model you are presented with, be realistic about what you can afford. If someone truly believes in you and feels inspired by the possibilities, they will work with you to find solutions. Just remember they need to eat too.

When you do find a manager that you feel could be a great fit, spend some time with them and get to know them before signing an agreement.

I NEED A BOOKING AGENT

Booking shows is a time-consuming and difficult process. And pitching yourself is an art form. Not every artist is good at pitching themselves, and they often need someone to help them with it. And just like when you might feel you need a manager, you'll think, "If I only had a booking agent, I'd have enough money flowing in from shows, and I'll finally be getting somewhere." And yes, a booking agent can be very helpful in growing your audience. But again, you have to ask yourself if a booking agent can actually "sell" you. Are you ready for market? Do you have the proper assets to help them do their job? What's in it for them? Do you have a clear audience to market to? Is your live show ready? Can you sell tickets? Will people actually come to your show? These are the questions the agent has to ask themselves before partnering with you.

If the answer is no to any of those questions, then you're not quite ready for an agent. You'll need to be the agent. You'll need to spend time building your network and researching venues that are a good fit for your music and your audience. You'll need to develop your assets so that you can cold pitch to a talent buyer (venue, festival, etc.) and make the impression you're trying to make. Be honest and authentic always. Be respectful and kind. And concise! Don't send very long-winded emails. If they don't know you, they won't take the time to read it. Be concise and clear about who you are, what you do and why they should consider booking you. Remember to ask yourself: What's in it for them?

You could be really great at pitching yourself and get some great shows. Some talent buyers really like dealing with the artist directly. I recommend you DIY it as long as you possibly can. Learn how to get really good at it. But if it's not in your comfort zone, that's okay too. There will be some levels of the business you will not be able to access without an agent, but get as far as you can on your own. Getting the help when it comes will be a welcome relief and will free up some time to focus on your craft. So work hard to create something an agent can carry forward for you to grow.

So, how do you know if you're ready for an agent? Well....when you have a show to sell. When your marketing materials (bio, website, socials, one sheet) all look professional and you can clearly communicate the experience of your show and what you charge for it. When you have a few key performances under your belt. When you can prove that you're a pro. That you are serious about what you do, that you're consistent and can be relied on to show up.

When you are ready for a booking agent, it's one of the simpler relationships you'll have on your team. The financial compensation for an agent is a little more clean in that they are only paid a percentage of the income they generate for you through booking shows, which is good. A booking agent is its own thing. Strictly speaking, managers don't book shows. Sometimes when you're starting out, a manager might do some of that job, but as you grow, you will need a separate person to do that job. These days, there are more and more hybrid smaller agencies where you can get a lot of artist services in one place: management, booking, label services, marketing, etc. This can be great, but make sure you really like the people you're working with before you move everything under one roof.

Finding the right agent doesn't require the same level of commitment as cultivating a relationship with a manager. Agents aren't involved in the vision for your career so much; they mostly execute show opportunities for you. But you should still be vigilant in choosing a good fit for you because you still need a champion. It's a very competitive space out there, and every artist needs their champions. No matter what level of the business they are at. You want an agent who is going to champion you and your music. Hopefully, one with a good network and some weight in the industry so they can get you higher profile shows. Do you research, look at their roster, years of experience and successes. Don't be shy to reach out to another one of their acts (if they have multiple) and start a conversation. It's helpful to have an agent who understands life on the road and will book with self-care in mind. That approach to touring is not always the most profitable, but it's really important that your champion has your wellbeing in mind, not just the money side of things. You also want to have confidence that when your agent is representing you, they reflect the same values you have. If kindness and respect matters to you, find an agent that will speak to others with kindness and respect.

When adding anyone to your team, always ask yourself, what do I bring to the table in this partnership? How will this agent benefit from working with me? Be clear in your own mind about what kind of agent will fit well in your team and then work hard to create a show that will be easy for them to sell.

I NEED A PUBLISHER

A publisher's job is to get songs into the marketplace. They essentially buy and sell songs and build catalogs. As a music creator, when you start out, you are your own publisher. Automatically. When you write a song, you own your writer share and publishing share until you choose to sign it over to someone else. Having a partnership with the right publisher can bring many opportunities for you. They will facilitate co-writes, pitch your songs to other artists, pitch your music for sync (music in TV/film/gaming/commercials, etc.) and help with the development of your craft as a writer. The right publisher can be a great sounding board for you as you expand and develop your gift of writing.

Publishers make their money from the income your songs generate. It used to be common to get signed to a publisher and get a draw - a monthly allowance for you to live on so you could quit your day job and write songs. That draw would be paid back with the income your songs generate. The changes to the economic structure of the music industry have seriously impacted publishing income. When we used to buy physical albums, the publishers would make money through licenses, but those licensing fees have diminished greatly due to streaming. As a result, getting signed to a publisher and getting a draw is a lot less common. Simply because there is not enough money floating around. The chances of the publisher recouping that money from your work is significantly lower. But even without a draw, a partnership with a publisher can yield a lot of benefits. It's one more champion working to get your songs out into the world. And if they are indeed a champion for you, that will bring good things. There are different splits when it comes to working with a publisher. I always recommend holding on to as much of your publishing as you possibly can, and a 50/50 co-pub deal is much more popular these days. If an opportunity presents itself, do you research, and don't be shy to ask questions. Remember that when you sign away a portion of your publishing, you're giving away cash. When and if you have commercial success with your music, a portion of that income will now go directly to your publisher. Be mindful of who you are giving it to.

There are more and more scams at the indie level when it comes to publishing. I see a lot of contracts that come to my clients. Every offer is something that you should weigh. But be vigilant. Try to stay clear of wording like "exclusive" and "in perpetuity." Exclusive means they would now be the only publisher working the songs (or a song if it's a single song contract), and in perpetuity means forever. A non-exclusive with a set term is always better because it gives you a point in time to get out, the chance to re-negotiate and the opportunity to have more than one person working your catalog. Like everything in business, there's a trade. Be clear about what you are trading and why.

I NEED A PUBLICIST

Publicity is a really interesting part of the music business, and it has changed so much with the digital age. A traditional publicist has relationships with mainstream media outlets, and when you engage a publicist on a contract, you are essentially buying access to those relationships and someone to represent you during that press cycle. Some publicists are amazing - they've been doing it for a long time, and they can get you and your music in key places for maximum exposure. It can be pricey, so you'll have to weigh whether it's the right fit for you. But if you're going into it thinking, "This is what I'm supposed to be doing" or, "This will help me get famous," those are not good reasons. It's important to have realistic expectations of what a publicity campaign will do for you and how much you should really spend on it. These days, a well-strategized Facebook or Google campaign can sometimes do more for you than a mainstream media campaign because you can focus your target audience. You will also have a lot of specific data to work with, which can inform future ad spends, whereas mainstream media campaigns will give you general impressions but not the data i.e. demographics, engagement, etc.

A publicist's job is to help you tell your story to the world. And "artist releases new music" is not a story. It might feel really important to you, but it's not really a news story. Unless you're famous. If you're famous, you're not reading this book. If you are just coming up and you're trying to build an audience, there needs to be more reasons for someone to care. Telling your story involves sharing more about who you are, your life, your reasons for making music, etc.

Now there are also digital publicists who are less expensive than traditional ones, and they pitch your story/new music to blogs, playlists and other digital spaces. This can be very useful because it drives the SEO (search engine optimization) on your name, provides you with quotes or reviews you can use in your promotional materials and so on. When you get spots in mainstream media, it does signal that you have reached a certain level, but in truth, it's more about what you can afford.

Remember that it's always about going fishing for your people. Finding and building your audience. So your decisions around whether you need a publicist and which kind to use should be based on seeing a direct line connecting what you do and where your people are. Sometimes it feels good to say, "I was on ETalk," but it's a lot of money to spend just to be able to say that if it doesn't convert to anything tangible for you in terms of fan base.

I NEED A RADIO PROMOTER

Radio promotion is a world unto itself, and the role of radio has changed over the decades. Radio is no longer a clear path to "breaking" an artist. It takes a lot of spins on a new artist to get any traction, and it's expensive. Artists signed to major labels will get most of the spins on commercial reporting radio stations. If you are an indie, commercial mainstream radio is not accessible to you in the same way. If you have a good relationship with a local commercial station, you may be able to squeeze into any local spotlight programming that exists with them, but we are seeing less and less connection between artists and commercial radio in their communities.

Community and college radio could be a great fit for you depending on what kind of music you make, but keep in mind that any radio love you get at this level, though wonderful support, won't do a lot to move the needle for you.. It will give you some great social media content and something to talk about, but one add at a college radio station won't be enough to create momentum on its own. But every add and every spin can be a puzzle piece to help the bigger picture of building your audience, and leveraging every opportunity is good business on your part.

Hiring a radio promoter or radio tracker might be a good fit for you, but it's a considerable expense with no guarantees. A tracker will pitch your track to radio and try to get it added or in rotation. A promoter will work the track and their relationships with music/program directors to get adds but also spins, helping the song to move up a chart or get the artist more exposure.

It'll cost thousands of dollars to work with a radio promoter or tracker, and if they are not pitching to reporting stations, you will likely not see any back end money from royalties. So it's money flowing out with no clear path on what you're buying, other than to say, "My song is on the radio." Which is fun to say and feels very validating, but as far as straight up business goes, it won't do a lot for building your audience or name recognition until you reach the commercial radio level. Which is very difficult without a major label behind you because radio wants to invest in an artist, not just a song. They want to know you're in it for the long haul. And if a bigger label is involved, it inspires confidence that the artist is one to bank on.

You can do a lot of radio work yourself - it will cost you time but not money. If you are planning a tour, contacting radio in the markets you'll be playing is always a good idea. But you can also do that yourself. It takes time, and you need to build your contact lists, but it's worth the effort. Local stations will sometimes have spots reserved for indie acts, or if they can't add your track, they may have a spot for community news on their website, that kind of thing. Working with radio where it makes sense is good. Expecting radio to make you a star is where you'll get frustrated.

The radio tracking world is full of people who will gladly take your money and make some calls for you. There is no guarantee of getting you adds. So do your research. A lot of research before working with a tracker. And most importantly, align your expectations. Be clear on why you're doing it, and position yourself to leverage any activity in the best way possible.

I NEED A PRODUCER

Finding the right producer match for you as an artist is a really important and special process. Firstly, make sure you are hiring a producer and not just an engineer. Engineers are wonderful, and their job is to capture the sounds you are creating with the right microphones and mix all that beautiful sound together. They don't usually consult on the arrangements or players or overall budget. When you hire an engineer, typically you are acting as the producer.

But when you hire a producer, they contribute to the overall artistic vision of the record. They oversee the timeline and budget as well. They find the right players, if needed, and pour their creative energy into the "sound" of the record. Some engineers are producers, and some are not. Some producers are engineers, and some are not.

Engineers are typically paid a studio rate by the hour and sometimes a flat rate. Producers are typically paid a rate per track/project, and they sometimes ask for points, meaning a percentage of the income the master recording makes. Sometimes producers will reduce their normal fee in exchange for points. Every deal is unique. Really well-established producers have their set pricing. They'll charge a certain fee for labels and another fee for indie artists.

If you, as a creator, are very confident in your arranging skills, or you have a band already and you work out the arrangements together, you might only need an engineer, and you could act as the producer. But if you don't have a clear idea of your "sound" and need someone to provide guidance there, you'll need a producer. Take your time finding one. Do your research. You want someone you can afford, someone with credentials. You'll want to listen to their reel, which will highlight their work. When you do, listen for sounds that you really want your record to have, and that way you know it's in their wheelhouse. Call up people who have worked with them before and ask what the experience was like. It can be intimidating going into the studio, so you want to choose an environment where you feel free to be totally yourself artistically. You want to work with someone who will listen to you when you try to explain the sounds that live in your head, someone open-minded and willing to work with you until you're happy with the sound. Music is a language in and of itself, so trying to explain what you hear in your head is a little like asking someone to explain what English sounds like. You might say, "I want it to sound a little more blue," but to someone else, your blue is their orange. You want a producer who takes the time to know your "blue." You want to work with someone who is patient and considerate. Especially if you're new at the recording process.

With the right producer, the recording process can be very rewarding. And a bit addictive as well. Hearing something you created come into the world with the added touches of another creator can be exhilarating. It can be equally as devastating when it goes wrong - you've spent all the money you saved and you're not happy with the sound. Sadly, this happens a lot. It comes down to communication and your own education on the recording process. Don't rush the process because you feel like you just have to get something out there.

The music industry is filled with wonderful helpers. But there are also lots of "industry people" who are trying to make their own living off your hopes and dreams. Those are the dangerous ones. The best way to protect yourself from those who prey on new and developing artists is to arm yourself with knowledge and look at everything from a business standpoint.

Ask a lot of questions if someone offers to "help." Check references. And don't get blindsided by famous names. Just because someone played guitar for Def Leppard in the 80s does not mean they are a producer, let alone the right producer for you. Name dropping is common practice in the industry. There's a difference between communicating who you've worked with to a prospective client and dropping names to sell yourself.

If someone drops names constantly, it's a red flag. Especially early on in your interactions with them. Music business professionals who have effected real change in people's careers rarely drop names. It's the same concept as very rich people not talking about money. They don't have the need to wave it around and spend in outlandish ways to show off that money. People with real money tend to be quiet about it. People with real music industry influence and experience are more quiet about it. They will spend more time asking you questions about yourself and your vision then they will spend telling you about what they've done or who they've worked with. The legit industry people will be excited about your music and the possibilities. They will cost money, don't get me wrong, because they need to make a living too. But their focus will be very different from someone trying to take advantage of you to keep their bills paid.

ASK YOURSELF

When you're finding your helpers, remember the KNOW, LIKE, TRUST guide.

1. Do you know them? Are you familiar with their work or the people they've worked with? Are they credible? Are they known in the industry? Known by people you trust?

2. Do you like them? Do you enjoy their company? Would you have them over for dinner with your family? Do you enjoy spending time with them? Are they generally likable? Liked by the people you like?

3. Do you trust them? Do your instincts say green light? Do other people trust them? Are they true to their word? Do they follow through on what they say? Are they credible?

As Meatloaf said, two out of three ain't bad. But ideally, you want a yes for all three.

CHAPTER 7
CAUGHT IN A TRAP

 They muddy the water to make it seem deep."

~ FRIEDRICH NIETZSCHE

Key Takeaway: Here we cover some common industry words that can trap you in a way of thinking that does not serve you.

There are a handful of words and common phrases related to the music industry that contribute to the sense of mystery. Some are often at the heart of the internal battle we have as creators. They perpetuate a misunderstanding of the music business, and they can trigger the part of ourselves that needs to be "chosen," deemed "worthy" and just "seen."

Some of these are used intentionally over and over to create the smoke and mirror illusions the big money industry requires to keep the power imbalance tipped in their favor. We are constantly fed the messaging that you need to be discovered to be successful. Audiences love the Cinderella story. We have so many TV shows about it. Listen to the language around it. For example, American IDOL - idol, someone to be revered, bowed down to. THE Voice - the one person who cuts through and is heard above the rest. The LAUNCH - the process that will shoot you to stardom. We are bombarded by this messaging in mainstream music industry media. No wonder we're all walking around waiting for someone to discover us. We're told over and over that's how it happens.

Now don't get me wrong, I am a business woman and I love the music business. I love making money. Money is not evil. It's just an expression of energy/vibration like everything else. And I believe most people get into the music business for the love of music. There are some bad apples and horrifying stories of artists being taken advantage of by powerful industry people, but for the most part, labels, agencies and other business entities in music are filled with people who are or were musicians, love songs and love music creators.

But when the industry leverages this illusion of needing to be discovered to be successful, to earn a living, it's often at the expense of the talent aka people, humans that are drawn to these so-called opportunities. And the result is disillusionment, anger and heartbreak. It's really important to understand that talent discovery programs, competitions, etc. are designed for one thing: the audience. If it's a television show, its main purpose is to serve the network's needs. Ratings. Audience size. It's not about you, the artist, at all. Some of my clients will argue that at least it's exposure and their name will get out there, and yes there is some truth to that.

But the audience are fans of the SHOW first. It's not easy to migrate that audience over to your own fan base. They love the feeling of being part of the Cinderella story. Once she marries the prince and lives happily ever after, who cares? Why stay with the story? The name recognition might help you start something, but you'll still be starting something from the ground up, and that's if you don't win. If you win, you'll be contractually bound and at the mercy of what's decided for you.

It's not only shows or talent competitions that can be a trap. Common music industry language can keep you stuck sometimes. Here are some of the words to watch out for and how you can take your power back by shifting their meaning.

SIGNED

Definition: To be contractually tied to a music entity such as a record label, publishing company, management or booking agency.

Illusion: I am chosen. I am worthy. I am legit. I have made it. I will be famous. I will be rich.

Think: If you have been chosen, then by whom? If you've been deemed worthy, by whom? And who gave "them" that power? If and when a contractual business partnership with a label or agency makes sense for your business, then fantastic. But you were worthy going into it, and you are legit before and after. Separate being "signed" from being "chosen" or "worthy."

Remember: Signed just means contractually obligated. It means you are in an agreement on paper to provide something in exchange for something else. It is completely separate from being worthy. It does not equal being famous or rich. It's just paper. You do not need a third party to determine that you and your music matters. Are you breathing? If the answer is yes, then you matter.

MAKING IT

Definition: Becoming a star? Getting somewhere? I don't really know, but I hear this all of the time, and I'm always like, "Make what?" What is IT?

Illusion: I will rise above and be seen. I will be admired. I will arrive.

Think: The problem with this is that there is no "there." There is no final arrival or destination point where you can declare having "made it.". Because we are always in motion. And as a creator, you will always want to create over and over, asking yourself, what's next?

Remember: Ask yourself, what does "making it" look like to you? Is getting signed "making it"? Bad news for you, if you do sign, it's only the beginning of the really, really hard work! Is a sold out global stadium tour "making it"? And what part of that vision is the "it"? Money? Fans? Fame? All of the above? Make these words work better for you and claim them. Define and name your "it," and then focus your intent to achieve it.

STAR

Definition: An individual who rises to fame and shines above the rest.

Illusion: I will be free to do whatever I want, whenever I want. I'll be powerful. People will look "up" to me.

Think: If you watch very famous people closely, more often than not, they say a life in public is anything but freeing. It can be quite isolating. But yes, your name recognition and brand can position you to help others, and in that way you have some leverage which you can use for good. But there is a massive trade-off - your freedom to move around anywhere in the world.

Remember: You don't need to be famous to make a living with your music. You can make money and still go to the store to buy milk. To be a star, all you have to do is shine....and you can do that every day, all day, being your own powerful self. It comes from inside you, not outside. It's in the allowing, letting who you are shine through.

FOLLOW YOUR DREAMS

Definition: Going after something you want, not letting anything stop you, having a vision for your life.

Illusion: You're asleep, and one day you'll wake up and have to get a real job.

Think: When I hear someone say, "I'm so happy you're following your dreams," it always causes me to pause. Aren't we all supposed to be doing that? Isn't that the point of life? Having joy and purpose in all things? To give vision to your life? And for some reason it comes up most often around the choice to build a career in the arts. Like it's some candy floss, pink and purple fluffy thing. It's very, very challenging to build a career in music. It is not rainbows and unicorns. I find this phrase particularly dismissive because it implies that one is asleep. We dream when we are sleeping. Meaning we should not be taken seriously when following our dreams, and the journey will end at some point when you "wake up to reality."

Remember: The next time someone says something along these lines, you can say, "The Matrix was a documentary, and you, my friend, are the one sleeping." Ok, maybe not that harsh, but you get the idea. Follow your dreams - your DAYDREAMS....eyes wide open, fully awake to all the possibilities. Follow the vision you have for yourself. Let your imagination run wild. Where does your mind drift off to? Where does it wander? Go there. For that is your soul calling out to you, showing you the way.

THE IT FACTOR

Definition: That special something that makes you a star.

Illusion: No one seems to be able to define it. Apparently it's a gut instinct declared by an industry professional. It's the "thing" that gets industry and fans excited about you and your music. It's a feeling.

Think: I believe there is such a thing as the "it" or "star" factor, but I believe it comes from inside. It's not determined by someone else claiming you have "it." It's like electricity or a charge - it's a frequency that you emit when you are in alignment with your authentic self, when you are connected to the source and you shine because you love what you do and are confident in that knowing. That resonance is attractive, and people are drawn to you, which in business terms equals money. Experienced music industry people have a radar for it. And because it comes from inside you, you have the power. It's not about someone else deciding it for you.

Remember: Only you can turn on your "it" factor by being in alignment with your authentic self. Knowing who you are and what you want without any doubt creates that vibe, and you will draw to you the helpers you need to get where you want to go. Be unapologetically YOU.

PLAN B

Definition: The plan you will eventually turn to when following your dreams doesn't work out.

Illusion: Plan B is the plan that makes everyone else around you feel better.

Think: Being a responsible adult is a good thing. I think it's important to be realistic about what it takes to build a sustainable business in music. But introducing a plan B, a fallback, does you a disservice because it implies failure right out of the gate. If you set off on your venture with a plan B in your back pocket, you've set the tone. You've invited failure into the mix.

Remember: If you need to, create a side by side plan. Music doesn't make money right out of the gate, and you need to eat. It's okay to have a sensible plan to survive in the world while you build your business. But shift your focus and see them as side by side plans. Not a backup plan. Managing the plans concurrently in a sustainable way makes sense, and it doesn't introduce a mindset of possible failure.

HIT SONG

Definition: A song that makes big money; a career maker.

Illusion: A hit song is impossible to predict, "lightning in a bottle" as they say, and you can't capture it on purpose. You just have to believe it's out there, hold on to hope and wait until you get a "hit" because it's not possible to be successful without a hit song.

Think: To me, a hit song is an accelerator, like fuel. It can help you move faster toward your goals. As an indie, it's like driving a car, and your "hit" song will be like horsepower, giving you a charge of momentum, accelerating you faster than before. But like anything, you need to know how to navigate at that speed to arrive somewhere significant. You also have to know where you are headed to get yourself there. A hit song as an indie will open doors for you; it will create opportunity. It'll draw attention like speeding down Main Street. Your fans will talk about it; they will share it more than other songs, and it will get more views, more likes, etc. Most importantly, it could help you get where you want to go a little faster.

If you are signed to a major label, you are likely sitting in a rocket. A powerful machine with the potential to reach the stars - you're sitting there, waiting for your rocket fuel. And a hit song or a hit record - that's the rocket fuel. The major labels know exactly how to drive that machine, and you are a passenger holding on for the ride, trying not to vaporize when you hit the stratosphere or come crashing down to Earth.

Remember: If you do have a "hit" as an indie, knowing how to maximize that opportunity is key. Otherwise, if you don't know where you are headed and you don't know how to drive at that speed, you will likely crash and burn, or the fuel will run out before you are able to use the opportunity to move to your next level. Prepare for a hit song and its potential. You'll know when you have one because it takes on a life of its own.

HYPE

Definition: Manufactured excitement about you and your music.

Illusion: Hype is exactly that, an illusion. Hype is when people likely to benefit from the artist or their music's success tell people how great the artist is. Hype can be a career killer. If you and your music are built up in a manufactured way and then people don't get their own excitement about it, there is no natural momentum, and it dies. Hype is orchestrated and needs constant fueling by some source i.e. advertising, money, etc. What you want is buzz.

Think: Buzz is organic and infectious. It's the electricity in the words people use when they are excited about an artist or their music. It's the motivation to tell someone else. Buzz is the excitement of discovery and the need to tell someone about it. Buzz is the most powerful indicator and validator for you and your music. When people are genuinely, without prompting, excited and talking about you and your music, it not only feels amazing, but it is super important for career growth. Buzz is everything. And knowing how to nurture buzz is an important skill. You cannot manufacture true buzz.

Remember: You can't force the love of your music. You can market it well and align your brand so that people understand you and your music, but you can't force the excitement. You can, however, be an example of excitement. If you are sincerely overflowing with excitement about what you create, it will spill over. Being excited about what you create is very different from being excited about the idea of what your creation might bring you i.e. fame and money. "Look I made a song, I'm going to be famous" feels very different from "Look at this song! I love this song. I can't believe this came through me. Listen to this song!"

Buzz starts with you and the love you have for what you are doing. Not where it will take you.

YOUR BIG BREAK

Definition: An incredible opportunity that causes you to break out - to rise from mediocrity. Your one chance to become a star.

Illusion: You only get that one precious chance to make it big. And if you miss your big break, you are doomed to a life of "I could have been a big star."

Think: How does it make any sense that you only get one chance for success? That kind of thinking only makes sense when you subscribe to the belief that someone else determines your fate. That someone else with more power than you decides whether you can live the life you envision for yourself.

Remember: Only you have the power to make the life you want. You can make choices every day to help build your success. There is not one big break. It's lots and lots of little breaks. Doors that open and that you choose to walk through. It's a constant layering of the choices you make and then stand upon to rise.

Words are powerful. They can be limiting or liberating. Be mindful of the language you use and the language that resonates with you. Watch for signs that you might be giving your power away. Don't chase. That's the trap. When you are chasing something, you're not paying attention to what's around you. You're focused on the chase. That's when it's easy to fall into traps. Stand firmly on the ground with your head up, taking it all in and watching. Look for your path, where the next step leads. Slow and steady she goes. Don't fall for the illusions. Create the magic instead. For your audience.

ASK YOURSELF

1. How do these industry buzz words resonate with you?

2. Become the observer of your mind. Are you running? If so, are you running toward something? Or away from something? What are you chasing?

3. Notice the pattern in the words you use. What do you believe about yourself and your music? What are your words telling you?

CHAPTER 8
PURPOSE IN ALL THINGS

> *Live with intention. Walk to the edge. Listen hard. Practice wellness. Play with abandon. Laugh. Choose with no regret. Appreciate. Continue to learn. Do what you love. Live as if this is all there is."*
>
> ~ MARY ANNE RADMACHER

Key Takeaway: Focused intent creates momentum; how knowing your why helps with clarity; building your audience means focusing on who's going to care about what you do.

One of the most challenging parts of being an artist and building a successful business with your music is having a clear vision of what you want. Getting in touch with what you actually want sounds easy, but it's often not. We are so conditioned by our upbringing, our schooling, our culture and community, too often driven by others' expectations of us that it is difficult to move forward in the understanding of our own desire. That part was really hard for me. I was so used to living for everyone else that I had no sense of my own internal compass, my own North Star. It took a lot of realigning for me to uncover what I actually wanted - for me. My own individual desires and vision for my life.

So many artists I consult with find themselves in the same situation. No clarity on their vision. Stuck in a loop. They go around and around and end up in the same spot, never seeming able to move forward past a certain point. They start all energized and creative and go-go-go and then, when what they hoped would happen doesn't happen because their expectation and outcome didn't line up, they fall down-down-down. They feel low, exhausted with not enough motivation to pick themselves back up and try again.

Having purpose in all things is vital to success. Focused intent creates momentum. And understanding your motivation will help you create the life you want for yourself.

WHAT'S YOUR WHY

I remember the first time I asked a client, "What's your why?" as in, "What's motivating you right now?" It quickly became a catchphrase that I use over and over in working with artists and songwriters. Understanding what motivates us to want something and take the steps to achieve it is critical to the understanding of ourselves. And it also helps to navigate expectations because your <u>in</u>tent becomes your <u>out</u>come - what you "house" aka "tent" inside you comes out. As within, so without. Understanding ourselves and why we want to do something is key to success.

Let's say a client says to me, "I want to release a single," and I say, "Ok, great! What's your why?" Usually at this point they stare at me blankly, and their answers vary from "'Cause that's what I'm supposed to do as an artist?" to "Because my friend did, and they got a million views!" At that point, I gently encourage them to look a little deeper. What outcome are you hoping for? When you imagine this in your mind, what does it look like? What's the emotion driving this thought/belief? These kinds of questions really help get to the root of the motivation.

This process requires a lot of honesty and the willingness to see yourself clearly and truthfully. That can be very scary for a lot of people. Understanding what is motivating you helps weed out potential pitfalls and helps align the outcome. Connecting your desire to the belief, the expectation and, most importantly, the emotion that's fueling it gives you the insight to navigate your decisions wisely. The spectrum of emotions ranges from negative to neutral to positive - any emotion rooted in the negative i.e. insecurity, fear, anger, etc. will yield a negative outcome, and positive emotions i.e. eagerness, anticipation, wonder, delight, ambition, excitement, etc. will yield a positive one.

So let's say you write a song, and you have a strong desire to record it. There could be a whole slew of reasons why you would want to do that. If your why is, "'Cause it'll make me famous," this is how we would get underneath that:

Why do you want to release a song? Because it'll make me famous.

Why do you want to be famous? I'll be rich, and my problems will go away.

Why does being rich make your problems go away? I can do anything and go anywhere, and I won't have as much stress.

So, you want to feel more freedom? Yes, being rich and famous gives me freedom.

So you want to release this song because success with it will lead to more freedom?

We would likely then have a discussion to recalibrate the belief that being rich and famous gives you freedom. There are many famous people who would argue the opposite. We would also likely go through an exercise to readjust the belief that releasing one song as an independent artist makes you rich and famous because it's not very likely.

The overall point is that taking the time to dive into your "why" reveals a lot about what you believe and what you seek. And when you break it down, we are always, without fail, trying to feel "better." We are always reaching to feel better, thought by thought, moment to moment. When we have a good feeling, we want to stay with it. When we have a not good feeling, we look for relief. Something that will help us feel better.

Being clear about your "why" is really important no matter how trivial or how big the decision you are pondering. The more aligned and clearer the intention, the more likely the outcome is positive because everything starts in your mind. What you think, you become. Thoughts turn to things. And you are the creator of your life, your reality. What you think and feel is driving your unique experience of life. The more dialed in you are, the clearer the signal, so always ask yourself, "What's my why?"

WHO CARES?

On first read, the words "who cares" always sound harsh to me. So negative. But if you change the inflection and emphasize the "who" instead of the flippant and dismissive negative tone, we get a clearer question. It's an important question, and the answer to it provides clarity and focus for your motivation. The first answer should be "me"; I care about this. I care about the music I'm making. I care about my show. I care about the fan experience of my show. And from there you expand outwards....who else is going to care about my music? If you create tailgating, beer drinking country music, who is going to care about that? Who is going to listen? If you create opera music, who is going to care? Who will enjoy listening to what you create?

My clients will often resist this process at first, saying things like, "My music is for everyone" or "I don't want to limit my potential." This process is not about limiting anything - it's about focus. It's about starting somewhere. Because as fans, we do listen to all kinds of music, and it is possible that a country music fan will also listen to opera. But a spillover audience is not the same as a target audience. Start with your target audience, and if your music connects well with others and gets some buzz going, the ripple effect will pull others in. Just because you start with your target audience does not limit who will hear it. It just helps with your marketing, promotion plans and narratives.

Finding your fans is a lot like fishing. You choose your water - lake? Pond? River? Ocean? And that gives you a good idea of what you'll find there. So if you're after trout, you won't choose the ocean. Lake or river will yield a higher chance of catching trout. The only chance of catching trout I think. Are there saltwater trout? No idea. I'm not much of a fisherwoman. I just think the analogy makes good sense. Focus, Tara, focus.

Okay, then you choose your boat, your rod/line, your lure and your bait. All of these choices you make are ways to increase your chances of catching trout. Now, if you're all set up to catch trout, and you're out on the water on a beautiful sunny day, and the first catch of the day is a bass, you don't say silly bass, this is not for you, you shouldn't be here. You say, "I got one!" Now if you don't know whether you're looking for trout or bass or pike, then you equip yourself with what you think has the higher chance of catching any of them. And then you start to see a pattern...if I use this lure and this bait, I get a lot of bass...if I use that lure and that bait I tend to catch pike, etc...

Through trial and error, you start to see what is attracted to what.

Same with music...sometimes it is more difficult to define what we create and figure out who would care about it. So trial and error it is. Study the engagement you get, the comments you receive, etc. and start putting the pieces together. Those patterns or indicators will help you with your budget decisions, how to spend your promotion and marketing money. If you already have a good idea that your music will appeal to, let's say the hip hop community, you're not going to spend a lot of time or money promoting yourself on operalovers.com - it's not to say that someone who loves opera won't love your hip hop, but the likelihood of there being a bulk audience to bring over into your boat is fairly slim. You want to get as much ROI (return on investment) as you can...aka most bang for your buck.

Being clear on who your music might appeal to is tougher than it may sound. It takes time to get to know yourself and your audience. And as an artist, you are always expanding and growing too, which expresses itself in your music, and you will see that reflected in the audience you attract as well. It's about focus and clarity, not limitations. And that being said, there will always be surprises regarding who is drawn to you and your music. Human beings are unpredictable, and there's a reason the music industry is a gamble. We can use our best knowledge and still get surprised.

The Who Cares question is important to the marketing process, but it shouldn't dominate the artistic process. Creating music because you know there's a market for it is a strategy, but if it doesn't feed your soul or connect with you, it's not sustainable. You might make money faster, but you're setting yourself up to be stuck in a position where your audience keeps expecting songs about rainbows, and you never actually liked rainbows, and now you have to sing about rainbows. All the time.

Start with the creative…what makes you feel alive? What do you love to sing about? What kind of beats do you love to make? What makes you feel most connected to all that is? And from there, go fishing for an audience that loves it the way you do.

FOCUS IS KEY

Where focus goes, energy flows. Our minds are powerful engines, and when a thought connects to an emotion, it becomes a magnet drawing an experience into our lives or pushing one away. Be mindful of your thought patterns. And practice focusing. Meditation is the single most powerful tool to help with this, and there are so many types of meditation and ways to get there. It does not have to involve candles or chakras or even anything spiritual. Dedicating 15 minutes a day to sitting quietly with your mind and listening to a steady sound like white noise (brown noise, pink noise, depends on what frequency feels comfortable to you) and let your thoughts drift. Don't engage with them; just let them float by like clouds. You'll start to notice that some thoughts have an emotional charge to them. Try not to engage with those - acknowledge them and let them drift. Eventually, as you practice this every day, you will get to a place where your mind actually does quiet down and you feel suspended. Meditation shuts down the parietal lobe - the part of the brain responsible for distinguishing the outline of you, where your arm starts and ends, that kind of awareness. When you shut down that part of the brain, you experience one-ness. A feeling of connection to all that is…a feeling of blending with the vibration of the universe. Practicing that blend fosters a deeper connection with yourself and the world around you.

As a music creator, when you create, in a way you are channeling. Your mind is open in a way that allows new information to flow through you and into the world. Practicing the ability to focus will not only help you with an overall feeling of peace, but it will help your creation process as well.

Where we focus our attention is our attraction point. And how we feel about what we are focused on determines the push and pull. Learning to be mindful of the duality in every thought is also part of mastering focus. For example, if you are focused on the thought "I want a hit song," the very fact that you use the word "want" implies a lack. Meaning you want something you do not have, so you are lacking the thing that you want. You are focusing on the absence of it. And so you are going to keep attracting the absence of it.

That desire also involves something completely out of your control. We can't control if a song becomes a hit or not. The fans decide that. There are also a lot of variables….how that song gets to the marketplace, how much reach you have, industry gatekeepers, budget….etc. So focusing on the thought "I want to write a hit song" is only going to reinforce the lack of having one. So what can you control?

Asking yourself, "What's my why?" Why do I want a hit song? What do I think it will do for me? How will it make me feel? That kind of focus also helps uncover more truth. Why do you want to write a hit song? Answers will vary…because it will make money… because I'll be famous…because I'll be able to pay my rent….because a TikTok viral song will get me a record deal…they all come down to the same thing: because I will feel validated as an artist. I will feel successful. I will feel worthy. I will feel better. I will feel good.

If you shift your focus from "I want to write a hit song" to "I want to feel good about this song I write," that's where the magic begins and where your true power lies. Stay in the now and feel your way through it. Because if you write a song that feels good to you, it will likely feel good to others. It will likely connect with others, and if it connects with a lot of others, it could become a hit. Sit with that good feeling. Imagine playing that song with hundreds or thousands of people singing along with you. What will that feel like? If you focus on the feeling of it, that's a powerful attraction point.

The key is where you are focused. If you are focused on something that you do not have yet, the universe will match the signal you are sending: "I do not have this thing that I think I want." And the universe will mirror that: "You do not have this thing you think you want." Focus on feeling good about the song you're writing. And this is not a comment on the genre or emotion of the song. It's about the process. You can write a song about your grandmother passing away or create an exciting EDM track…you can feel good about either of those processes from a crafting standpoint. And if you feel proud and excited to share what you created with the world, the universe will match that: "We want to share this with the world. Okay, then let's get this out to the world."

Where focus goes, energy flows. Focus your intent, align your emotions around that intent and you can create any reality you want.

We are always creating our reality with our thoughts and emotions. The difference is moving from an unconscious creator to a conscious creator. And that all starts with awareness and then focus. Choose to feel good. Learn to sit with your emotions. Be curious about what you feel, when and why. Ask a lot of questions about yourself. Get to know yourself.

The basis of life is freedom. We have the freedom to choose our mindset every moment of every day. You are free to live however you choose. Everything starts in your mind. Your thoughts and beliefs. In any moment, you can choose how you want to feel simply by changing your focus.

The purpose of life is joy. Follow the good feelings. Choose joy. Choose to feel good. We are supposed to feel good in this life. We are here for the adventure of it all.

The result of life is expansion. We are here to grow and learn and expand in the experience of who we are and the remembering of where we come from. We are pure positive energy having a human experience. As a music creator, you are channeling creation through you into the world. That's why it feels so amazing to be a music creator.

Having purpose in all things will give you a sense of grounding. It shines light on your path. Being clear on your why makes you feel more sure-footed. It's worth the time to do the inner work so that the outer journey is more fulfilling.

ASK YOURSELF

1. Do you have a sense of your own internal compass? Can you clearly see and feel what you want for your life?

2. What is your why? Ask yourself that constantly as you get to know yourself more deeply.

3. Who will care about what you do? Who are your people? Where should you go fishing?

4. Are you able to focus your thoughts? Are you able to sit in silence with yourself?

CHAPTER 9
THE EXPERIENCE OF YOU

 Branding is what people say about you when you're not in the room."

~ JEFF BEZOS

Key Takeaway: Understanding what a brand is and how to develop your own brand identity; essential tools to help build your audience.

This is one of my favorite quotes about branding. I think it's a great way to explain this thing called a brand - a trendy word thrown around a lot on social media. And widely misunderstood. Let's start with what a brand is NOT. A brand is not your logo. Branding is not the colors you use on a website or the style of T-shirt you sell in your merch. Your website, logo and merch are all expressions of your brand.

A brand is a feeling.

It's the way something or someone makes us feel.

Think about a huge corporate brand for a minute. Let's make it McDonald's - a huge global brand. Whether you actually eat at McDonald's or not, if you were raised in North America, you have a sense of what McDonald's is all about. It's comfort food. Cheap, fast comfort food. If you ate there as a kid, your experience of MacDonald's will have warm fuzzy feelings around the memory of getting the toy in your McHappy Meal. Good feelings around laughing and hanging with your friends as a teenager there because it was the only takeout food you could afford. As parents, taking your kids there because it's easier than cooking after a long day at work. And they loved it. Win win. Comfort. Easy. Feel good.

McDonald's sells the feel-good feeling of tasty, addictive food that everyone can afford. The fact that the food is terrible for you health-wise is secondary. Even when you know the effects of too much McDonald's and fries that never rot (thank you Super Size Me!), we can still find a feel-good feeling about eating at McDonald's. Maybe not always, but even health gurus understand the draw of McDonald's - it becomes the cheat day. Comfort. Relief. Easy.

It's a powerful brand, and even when it was hit hard by a documentary that exposed the health risks, it came back stronger than ever. Because they understand the power of a brand and the psychology behind it.

You have a brand. I prefer to say brand identity because it reminds you to connect it to you, the person. Your identity. As opposed to it being something apart from who you are. Your brand identity is the experience of you. How people feel when they experience you, your music, your show, your social media content...any interaction with you. Branding is a story and the feeling that comes with it. It's the story you choose to tell the world about who you are, what you're doing and why you do it. It's how you communicate who you are in everything that you do.

Brand identity is a combination of your personal values, how you communicate those values, the experience of your product and what you want people to feel when they interact with your product. Essentially, your brand identity is the personality of your business combined with a promise to your customers aka fans.

Defining your brand - especially because in music, you, a human being, are the product - requires you to look inside yourself. In order to communicate who you are, you have to know who you are. It is a journey of self discovery. It is first an internal exercise and then an external one. Connecting what you know to be true about yourself with the world.

This process is about self-discovery and communication. NOT imitation. NOT manufacturing. Authenticity is the only path to successful branding. It's not about becoming something you THINK you should be. Becoming something other than yourself because it sells. It's about having a grounded sense of what's true about you, insight into what people enjoy about you and the skill to communicate that feeling in everything you do.

As humans, we are complex. We don't like being boiled down to one thing. And branding is not about just being one thing. Remember, it's the feeling of the experience of you. Let's look at major brands in music. What's the feeling that comes to mind when you think of them?

Taylor Swift: Power? Strength? Rebel?

Elvis Presley: Swoon? Dominance? Confidence?

Blake Shelton: Easygoing? Laidback? Country boy?

As you reach for feelings that describe major music brands, you start to see a consistent pattern in their brand….their songs, their shows, their merch. That personality thread runs through everything they do. And you come to expect a certain experience from them. You expect to feel in awe when you see Taylor's show. You expect a down to earth, simple I'm just living a simple life attitude with Blake.

Now, as people, we have more than one personality trait. We have many sides to us. Who we are with a romantic partner is different from who we are with our boss. (Unless you're dating your boss - sidebar, probably not a great idea.) The parts of ourselves we choose to show a stranger we're meeting for the first time are very different from the parts of ourselves we show our best friend. We are like kaleidoscopes. We shine from different angles depending on who's looking at us.

The trick to being successful with your brand identity in music is knowing which sides of yourself you want to show the world. If you are a heavy rocker, your brand is probably not going to be the softer side of you that rocks your baby to sleep at night. You'll want your brand to feel like your music. If you are a folk singer-songwriter, your brand is probably not going to have a night club party vibe. Your music will likely be more chill and acoustic. Focusing the feeling you want people to have in the experience of you is a conscious choice, yes. But it's not manufactured. It's just intent. And intent dictates the outcome.

If you are not intentional about your actions, the outcome will be chaos. If people don't understand who you are and what you're about, they are not likely to connect with what you do. If they don't connect, they don't buy. If you know how to create an emotional connection through the experience of you, and it's a good feeling for your fans, they will want to feel that way again and again, which equals a sustainable living for you.

We can't control what people think of us. We can't control people's experience of us. It's a complete waste of time to try. But coming back to Jeff Bezos' quote, you do want to have a sense of what people say about you when you're not in the room. Your brand identity is about trying to manage that outcome. Being aware of what the conversation in your absence might be. And being clear and consistent in every medium you use to communicate your desired messaging with your fans. Clarity and consistency is everything.

Notice the music you love. Notice what you come to expect from a new album release from your favorite artists. When we experience music we absolutely love, songs that make us feel something good, we hope and expect the artist to release something that will make us feel that way again.

So how do you develop and define your brand identity? Here is an exercise that will help you narrow in on the experience of you.

BRAND FOUNDATIONS - WHAT'S MY WHY?

1. List the top 5 artist brands you like or love AND what you admire about them.

2. List your top 3-5 values.

3. What is your mission? In other words, what do you want to do with your values?

4. What is your vision for your career?

5. Where do you see your career in 1 year, 5 years, 10 years?

FUNDAMENTAL NATURE - WHO'S GOING TO CARE?

1. Describe the nature of your music in one sentence.

2. List some similar artists to you.

3. What is unique about you versus these artists?

4. What is the primary differentiator between you and them?

PERSONALITY - THE FEELING OF ME

1. How would you describe yourself?

> (Energetic, Outgoing, Friendly, Attentive, Casual, Formal, Businesslike, Serious, Relaxed, Funny, LaidBack, Progressive, Calm, Authoritative, Warm, Capable, Masterful, Resourceful, Inventive, Proactive, Problem-solving, Trustworthy, Solid, Cutting Edge, Organic, Understanding)

2. Any additional words describing your personality?

3. If your music was a place, where would it be?

4. If your music was a vehicle, what would it be?

5. If your music was a bumper sticker or a quote, what would it say?

ELEMENTS - THE EXPRESSION OF ME

1. Are there images or icons that appeal to you that you feel reflect you and your music?

2. Are there colors that you feel resonate with you and your music?

3. Is there a particular tone to your average speech?

4. If you think of your music as a mood, what mood is it? What's the vibe? Describe it.

It's not an easy exercise, and it takes a few sessions with my clients to peel back the layers, so I'll give you a set of answers to help you based on me as an artist. The trick is not to overthink it too much. Don't try to be clever. Trust your first thoughts.

ARTIST: Tara Shannon

Brand Foundations - What's My Why?

1. List the top 5 artist brands you like or love AND what you admire about them

Jann Arden - her songwriting, her sense of humor, her stage presence

Céline Dion - her talent, her grace and commandment of the stage

Sarah Bareilles - her wicked sense of lyric and melody. I wish I could write like her

Ed Sheeran - his work ethic, determination and vulnerability he shares in his music

Annie Lennox - her voice, her timelessness, her individuality

2. List your top 3-5 Values

   - kindness
   - compassion
   - humor
   - respect

3. What is your mission? In other words, what do you want to do with your values?

   - to make music that helps people connect with themselves more deeply but also laugh at ourselves and this thing we call being human

4. What is your vision for your career?

   - build a sustainable living in all things music, creating it, sharing it and mentoring those who wish to do the same

5. Where do you see your career in 1 year, 5 years, 10 years?

   - In 1 year, touring in Canada/US with my new album

   - In 5 years, filling soft seat theaters across Canada in every major market

   - In 10 years, doing a few key shows per year, writing more books and educating and empowering other music creators around the world

Fundamental Nature - Who's Going To Care?

1. Describe the nature of your music in one sentence.

   Inspirational, country, soul that uplifts with its storytelling

2. List some similar artists to you

   Sarah McLachlan, Trisha Yearwood, Jennifer Nettles

3. What is unique about you versus these artists?

   Mother of seven kids, broader range in style

4. What is the primary differentiator between you and them?

My life experience and the stories I tell

Personality - The Feeling of Me

1. How would you describe yourself?

Warm, kind, relaxed, funny, trustworthy, strong minded.

2. Any additional words describing your personality?

Hopeful and positive

3. If your music was a place, where would it be?

Sitting under a Willow tree at the edge of a pond

4. If your music was a vehicle, what would it be?

Not a car, a magic carpet

5. If your music was a bumper sticker or a quote, what would it say?

Just wing it. Life. Eyeliner. Everything.

Elements - The Expression of Me

1. Are there images or icons that appeal to you that you feel reflect you and your music?

   Soft flowing lines, no sharp edges

2. Are there colors that you feel resonate with you and your music?

   Rose Gold

3. Is there a particular tone to your average speech?

   I have two distinct tones…wistful, calm and in love with life and a direct, intentional tone that comes out when I'm teaching

4. If you think of your music as a mood, what mood is it? What's the vibe? Describe it.

   The mood or vibe of my music is uplifting and inspiring in an easygoing, chill way

Hopefully through the answered version, you can start to see how my brand identity would look and feel. You might get an impression of what my music would sound like. Then go listen and see if it was a match! (www.tarashannonmusic.com - clever way to get streams, right?)

Once you do have that clear sense of who you are, what you have to say and how you want to say it, refer to it when you're prepping your show, when you're designing your merch, when you're posting on socials. Did you stay in line with your core messaging? The feeling of you? Or did you move away from it? When I create a post, I ask myself, does this feel like sitting under a willow tree by the edge of a pond on a magic carpet with a just wing it attitude? If it does, post away. If it doesn't, tweak it a bit so that it is consistent with your brand identity. If you're posting, it's because you're trying to drive followers. So do it well - the effort pays off. Be purposeful and mindful in the sharing of you.

There is only ONE you. The key to setting yourself apart in the competitive space that is the music business is to reveal the most authentic, truest version of YOU bravely to the world in a way that evokes emotion in others. A feeling of connection.

When you have a good handle on what you're about, what your music is about and the experience of you, you're in a much better position to intentionally and successfully build your audience.

FINDING YOUR PEOPLE

Building your audience will come from a combination of live shows, touring and digital marketing on social media platforms and YouTube. You can choose to focus only on touring if that's what appeals to you, and you can choose to focus all your efforts on content creation. It'll come down to what's motivating you. It's very difficult to break even as an indie artist with your live shows when you're starting out. But if you're okay not making money and you need the connection with the live audience, then it's a great fit for you. If you don't want to lose money out on the road, then learning about content creation and digital marketing will be a very effective way to build your fan base. These days, a hybrid approach combining live shows with a smart digital strategy seems to yield the best results, but it also depends on the type of music you make and how flexible your life is to allow for touring.

No matter what combination of strategies you choose, the psychology of building relationships remains the same. The strategies you use to build your fan base will be more effective if you understand the basics of how we as humans form relationships and the function of marketing.

Marketing: *The action or business of promoting and selling products or services; the process of attracting potential customers and clients to a product or service.*

Yes, this is true for music marketing. However, we do need to tweak it a little because the relationship between a customer and product (and the company that sells it) is very different from the relationship between fan and artist. Fan/artist connections feel more personal than product/consumer ones.

Let's say I need a broom. I'm probably going to either scroll on my phone to find one, check the reviews, the price, the delivery and make a decision. Or I might go to the store and choose the one that looks most appealing to me because of the design, the price, familiarity with the name brand, etc.

When I get the broom and use it, I'll either feel happy about my purchase, grateful for its usefulness or disappointed and frustrated if it's not what I hoped for. Then I would simply get another one. My relationship with the product and the brand pretty much starts and ends with my experience using the product.

But with fans, it's much more personal. There's an ongoing investment in the relationship. There's a feeling of loyalty, commitment, connection. When fans connect with our music, they feel seen and understood. They feel a kinship with the artist who created it. They feel gratitude and awe. It's a unique and special relationship. One that shouldn't be taken for granted and should be treated with the utmost care. It's difficult to build your fan base. It's easy to lose them if you're not managing the relationship with care. Taylor Swift is the most brilliant example these days of an artist who deeply cares for her fans. And they feel it. They know it. It's real and authentic and consistent. As a result, her legion of fans is massive. Her fans feel connected to her personally. She worked hard to cultivate that. It did not happen by accident, and it's an extension of who she is as a person. As an indie artist with a smaller fan base, you need to put the same heart and attention into your fan base. It might not be millions, but each and every one of them counts.

Fan relationships are committed relationships; interpersonal committed relationships as humans follow distinct stages.

1. **Introduction**: When we meet someone for the first time, this is the introduction phase. Hello, nice to meet you. My name is. That kind of thing. Small talk. We often talk about the weather because it's a common experience, and when we don't know anything yet about the person we are meeting, we gravitate to the common. Come here often? Referencing the common space you're in. Is it your first time

at this conference? Referencing the common experience of the event you're both attending and so on. At this stage, our brains are assessing whether the person we are introduced to is worth the energy and effort to move to the next stage. If something turns us off at the introduction stage, the relationship will not move forward. "Are you from Tennessee? Cause you're the only Ten I See." By-ee.

2. **Education**: If the introduction stage goes well and we feel some sort of connection, whether it be curiosity, interest, familiarity, any positive feeling really, we will open up to the education part. We will share more of ourselves. Give away information about ourselves. I live over in Richmond Hills. I'm a singer. I'm single. That kind of information. Anything that provides more knowledge about ourselves. We might find we have nothing in common, or maybe we don't like the things we learn about the person, so we'll start winding it down, deciding to not invest more time and energy into the conversation or relationship. If we do find we have things in common or feel a sense of connection, we'll move to the next stage.

3. **Permission**: This is where there is an exchange that signals permission to further the connection. You like golf? I'd love to have you at the club sometime. What's your number? I'll set up a tee time. You live just a few blocks over from me. We should go for coffee sometime. That kind of thing. A signal that says, you have my permission to keep developing this connection.

4. **Nurturing**: After the permission stage, you're in nurturing. Maintaining that relationship and the level of connection you experience from it. That one golf game turning into a regular weekly tee time. The one coffee meetup turning into a dinner date, etc., and

we can go backwards too. If you discover something you don't like once in the nurturing stage as you get to know someone, you can go back and set new boundaries around permission, share less and less information, and create space and distance so the relationship naturally fades away.

There are many more complexities, of course, but thinking in terms of these stages when it comes to your marketing to build a fan base is important. Understanding which phase you're in with your fans will inform your ask. If you're meeting someone for the very first time, you wouldn't say, "Hey, can I borrow your car?" We have social norms that tell us that would be inappropriate. It's too much too soon. There hasn't been enough time to establish trust or friendship. Asking a brand new fan just discovering you to pay a $10/month subscription fee will probably not be successful. Inviting a group of hardcore followers who have been your fans for years to VIP level access with exclusive perks with a fee of $10/month, now that'll work very well.

These strategies come into play when you're using digital ads and social media to build your audience, as well as any marketing materials you prepare at any given time. They are also important for the connection with your fans at live shows and how you approach your live show. If you're playing a venue for the first time as an opener for an established act, you're going to approach the set like you would approach someone you're meeting for the first time. It's going to have a "hey, I'm so and so and this is my music" kind of vibe. If you're playing to a sold out crowd in your home town and everyone is only there to see you, you're not going to start your show with "Hi, I'm so and on, here's some of my songs." You're gonna come out guns blazing ready to rock and roll. Just like seeing your best friend after months apart…it'll be all smiles and big hugs.

Building your fan base effectively starts with communicating your brand effectively - the experience of you and your music. Being able to do that, means you need to know yourself and feel a strong connection to the essence that is YOU. Always come back to you. Who are you? What do you have to say? And how do you want to say it?

Develop your statement of purpose. Here's the framework:

> I *(insert what you do)* for *(who you do it for)* through *(how you do it)*.

For example, my artist statement of purpose is:

> *I help people find their feel good through songs, stories and sit downs.*

Stay on brand with everything you do to build your music business, refer to your statement of purpose often and, most of all, maintain a strong connection to self firmly rooted in a deep sense of knowing who you are so that you can weather anything that comes your way.

ASK YOURSELF

1. Do I have a brand yet? Is who I am and what I am about clear in all my messaging as an artist?

2. Is there consistency across all my social platforms, my website, my music artwork?

3. What is my statement of purpose? What's my why? And who's going to care?

4. What have I discovered about myself recently?

CONCLUSION

 Music is a healing energy that connects us all and powers the human spirit."

~ TARA SHANNON

No matter whether you're a hobbyist or an indie artist trying to make your way or a signed artist with a major label, you are a music creator. And that's amazing. If your only audience is just your best friend - you matter and your music matters. If you are playing to thousands of fans - you matter and your music matters. Learn how to separate external affirmations from your internal validation; that's what will put you in control of your mindset and your emotions. Put you in the driver's seat. The seat of your soul. Always look inside yourself for that sense of validation. Strengthen your internal compass and point it to YOUR North Star. Even if no one else is traveling in that direction. Make your own path. Trust yourself. Remember there is only one you.

The business of music will continue to ebb and flow. The "best" strategy will always be changing. New technology, new social platforms, new ways to build your audience. You will best be able to adapt to those changes when you are on firm footing with yourself. The knowing of who you are and what you have to say with your music. And surround yourself with people who lift you up and make you a better version of yourself. From a place of confidence and clarity, you will be able to carve out a plan for yourself in any business environment. Able to weather any and all changes in the music industry space.

Stay curious. Stay informed. Sign up for reputable newsletters, join industry groups, go to industry conferences. Keep up to date with what's happening out there, but also keep up with what's happening inside of you. Find ways to stay grounded and inspired. Take time for self-care - whatever that looks like for you. Put your phone away and walk in a forest. Turn off notifications and read a great book. Exercise. Cook. Connect with friends. Find what works for you to help you stay connected to self. Remember to fill the well.

And dream. Look out to the world and dream up a vision for your life in your mind's eye that feels possible and excites you. But then turn your gaze inward because learning about yourself is how you will truly awaken so that you can start living that vision for your life filled with a sense of purpose.

Finding balance and joy as a music creator in today's music industry comes from understanding yourself as a person…from a deeper sense of self. From that place, you can navigate every area of the business with clarity and a better sense of purpose, which in turn brings you success.

Success doesn't come from chasing something outside yourself. Chasing who you think you should be. True and lasting success starts from inside you and is then expressed through you, because of who you are.

Understand you and you understand people - understand people and you understand business.

To be successful in the business of music, you first need to be successful in the business of YOU.

AUTHOR'S NOTE

This is YOUR life. Make it anything you want it to be. You love music! Lean in. It's a gift. Music is a gift. There are so many ways to receive music into your life. To fit making music into your life. Find the way that brings you the most joy...that makes you feel the most alive.

You have a vision for your life. Even if it seems as though there are so many obstacles between you and realizing that vision, don't lose sight of it. Keep the target locked on where you want to be. Open heart, open mind. Slow and steady. Step by step you will create that life you envision for yourself. Make no apologies for it. Don't explain yourself to anyone. You don't have to justify the life you want for yourself. It's your life.

Don't let the fear of what others might think of you weigh you down. It's none of our business what other people think of us. We have no control over that. We can only control our choices. Everything is a choice. What we think. What we feel. What we do.

Claim the right to live your life completely free. Free from the fear of being judged or misunderstood. I promise you that if you find the courage to step into the fullness of who you are, there is only joy that awaits. On the other side of fear is everything you've ever wanted for yourself.

The only thing that ever truly matters is the relationship between you & you. You and your inner being. How you feel about yourself. What you believe about yourself. Who you are as a person. And finding peace within. A deep connection with the essence of who you are. You are here to do great things. Your passions are the road map to that adventure. Follow your passion. Always.

YOU are a music creator.

So CREATE! With full abandon.

And LIVE! Your fullest life.

MEET TARA SHANNON

Tara Shannon is an award winning artist and songwriter with over 30 years of experience in the music industry. As a celebrated entrepreneur and founder of Willow Sound Records, Tara has been a guest speaker at notable events such as the G20 Summit and won awards such as the BMO for Woman Community and Charitable Giving. Tara seeks to encourage and empower the artists on her label roster with the same entrepreneurial mindset.

Tara also founded The (Gro)ve which offers one on one sessions in strategic planning, social media management, song coaching and performance coaching as well as general life coaching for music makers. With a special focus on empowerment through education, The (Gro)ve helps artists "gro" into their full potential.

As an artist, Tara Shannon's music has been described as soft rock/inspirational with plenty of soul and a voice to be heard.

Tara divides her time between Ottawa and Nashville and lives with her family in the village of Russell.

- Website: www.booktara.co
- Website: www.gro-ve.com
- Contact Willow Sound Records: admin@willowsound.com

EMOTIONAL CHECK IN

HOW DO I FEEL IN THIS MOMENT?

I FEEL GOOD

Whatever you're feeling good about at this moment, stay with it. Milk it for all it's worth. Soak it up. Good feeling thoughts mean you're connected with your inner being and you're in alignment with your authentic self.

I DO NOT FEEL GOOD

Bad feeling thoughts are an indicator. It's your inner being trying to get your attention because something you are thinking or believing in this moment is out of alignment with your authentic self. A negative emotion is your inner guidance system flashing a red light at you saying, "Look here - this is where you need to adjust your belief."

EMOTIONAL CHECK IN

This exercise can help you discover the core beliefs and underlying fears you might have that are affecting how you feel about yourself and your music journey.

Find a quiet place. Follow these steps.

EMOTIONAL CHECK IN

1. **How am I feeling?** *(Name the emotion)*
2. **Does it feel good?**

   Yes → Great! Lean in.
   No → Do you want to keep feeling this way?

   ↓

   Yes → Great! Lean in.
   No → Find the thought that's looping around in your head making you feel bad.

   What is the belief behind the thought?
   I believe _____.

   What is the fear?
   I am afraid that _____.

   And the answer will likely be rooted in one of these five root fears:

   Rejection. Humiliation. Abandonment. Injustice. Betrayal.

3. **Acknowledge the fear.**

4. **Challenge the fear with evidence from your life**.

What I believe about myself at this moment does not feel good, which is my inner guidance system telling me to adjust my belief. Where is the evidence in my life that says this is not true about me?

When you find the root of the fear and the core belief that goes with it, the feeling will dissolve…you will feel a sense of relief. By shining a light on why you're feeling the way you're feeling and responding to your inner guidance system trying to get your attention about something you believe that is out of alignment with the truth of who you are, you will feel better.

> Example:
> *How do I feel?* Anxious.
> *Does it feel good?* No
> *Do I want to keep feeling this way?* No
> *What's the thought?* No one is buying tickets to my show
> *What is the belief behind it?* I'll be playing to an empty room
> *What's the fear?* Rejection
> *Challenge the fear:* Does low ticket sales mean I am being personally rejected? No. The date, time, location and promo budget are all factors. My show is separate from "me." If no tickets sell, I'll do the best I can with my show and learn what to improve next time. *Where is the evidence in my life that I am not being rejected?* I played a show last week and 25 people came out.

MOOD INDEX

Use this index to find sections of the book that will help you feel better when you're stuck in a negative thought.

LIST OF THOUGHTS/BELIEFS
(these are some common ones that I see in my coaching)

I suck *(The Three Elements - page 19)*
I'm never gonna get there *(Conclusion - page 109)*
I'm running out of money *(Money Tree - page 53)*
No one is coming to my show *(Growing Your Fan Base - page 17)*
My songs suck *(It's All About The Song - page 42)*
I don't know what I'm doing *(What's Your Why - page 86)*
Someone said I'll never make it *(Making It - page 77)*
I don't have enough money to make music *(The Three Elements - page 19)*
I'm not making any money with my music *(Money Is The Life Blood - page 55)*

My parents told me to get real job *(Making It Your Business - page 22)*
I'm singing to an empty room *(Building An Audience - page 33)*
Radio won't play my song *(Radio Promotion - page 68)*
I have to get these songs out now *(Don't Be In A Rush - page 45)*
I saw another artist friend's post and now I'm depressed *(Your North Star - page 109)*
I'm not getting anywhere *(The Creative Cycle - page 11)*
I need a manager *(Helpers - page 62)*
I don't know where to start *(The Core Principles - page 27)*
I don't feel like doing anything today *(Drive - page 21)*
I am overwhelmed *(Focus Is Key - page 90)*
I need a record deal *(Indie. Redefined. - page 1)*
Business is too complicated *(Purpose In All Things - page 85)*
I'm not a sell out *(Focused Intent - page 35)*
I make art, I don't want to do business *(Being In Business - page 34)*
I just need my big break *(Your Big Break - page 82)*
I just need one hit song *(A Hit Song - page 80)*
I should have a plan B *(Plan B - page 80)*

RECOMMENDED READING

Cameron, Julia. The Artist's Way.

Dispenza, Dr. Joe. Becoming Supernatural.

Dodson, Marty. Song Building: Mastering Lyric Writing.

Dodson, Marty, Mills, Clay, and O'Hanlon, Bill. The Songwriter's Guide to Mastering Co-writing.

Dyer, Dr. Wayne. Change Your Thoughts, Change Your Life.

Gauthier, Mary. Saved by a Song.

Gladwell, Malcolm. The Tipping Point.

Herstand, Ari. How to Make It in the Music Business.

Housel, Morgan. The Psychology of Money.

Levitin, Daniel J. This is Your Brain on Music.

Miller, Donald. Story Brand.

Pattison, Pat. Songwriting Without Boundaries.

Singer, Michael J. The Untethered Soul.

Tolle, Eckhart. The Power of Now.

Thank You For Reading My Book

I really appreciate all of your feedback and I love hearing what you have to say.

I need your input to make the next version of this book and my future books the best they can be.

Please take two minutes now and leave a helpful review on Amazon letting me know what you thought of the book.

Thanks so much!

Tara Shannon

www.ingramcontent.com/pod-product-compliance
Lightning Source LLC
Chambersburg PA
CBHW052142070526
44585CB00017B/1931